A Path to
PEACE

A Path to
PEACE

George Sifri, MD

With Contributions by David Sifri

ARCHWAY
PUBLISHING

Archway Publishing books may be ordered through booksellers or by contacting:

Archway Publishing
1663 Liberty Drive
Bloomington, IN 47403
www.archwaypublishing.com
1 (888) 242-5904

Because of the dynamic nature of the Internet, any web addresses or links contained in
this book may have changed since publication and may no longer be valid. The views
expressed in this work are solely those of the author and do not necessarily reflect the
views of the publisher, and the publisher hereby disclaims any responsibility for them.

This book is a work of non-fiction. Unless otherwise noted, the author and the publisher
make no explicit guarantees as to the accuracy of the information contained in this book
and in some cases, names of people and places have been altered to protect their privacy.

ISBN: 978-1-4808-3404-0 (sc)
ISBN: 978-1-4808-3405-7 (hc)
ISBN: 978-1-4808-3406-4 (e)

Library of Congress Control Number: 2016913116

Print information available on the last page.

Archway Publishing rev. date: 11/4/2016

For my wife
Raye Ann
who encouraged me to listen with my heart
and to cherish each moment

Thanks for everything
I love you

This book is about love,
about reminding people of who they are,
a part of light—a part of God.
I am simply here to shake the branch,
the branch they have chosen to rest upon.
Like beautiful butterflies,
they pause momentarily before once again resuming flight,
and as I watch them depart,
I am in awe.

CONTENTS

Peace through Love

Connecting with God

Find and Express Your Truths

Staying Connected through Adversity

Surrendering to God

*   The spiritual messages in these chapters were received and transcribed by
     David Sifri.

FOREWORD

A Sunday school teacher walked into the classroom and asked the students, "If I gave you five hundred bucks, how many of you would not love your mother and father?" The room was silent until one little guy in the back row raised his hand. The teacher said, "Timmy, you would take $500 not to love your mother and father?" Timmy said, "No! But how much would you pay me not to love my sister?"

Ann Landers, a famous columnist in newspapers throughout the country, was asked in a letter, "When can I stop kissing my kids?" Ann Landers responded, "Never!" In the same column, she carried a story about a mother and father who wished they had shown more affection to their son. Their letter expressed their regret in not having done so—as they bent over his coffin to kiss him one last time.

So often, we take love for granted. We take the important others in our lives for granted. We go about our daily routines never taking the time to say "I love you!" and mean it. This book written by George Sifri is about love. However, if one reads the book from the perspective of physical love, one will be very disappointed. This book portrays love from a spiritual perspective. Each and every one of the stories is born from the realization of love. This love is present in the depth of every man and woman regardless of his or her religious affiliation, background, socioeconomic status, and life calling. It is this love that is synonymous with God, because from a biblical perspective, "God is love!"

Much of the book is born from lunch conversations between George, me, and countless others, coupled with George's beloved wife, Raye Ann, and the patients he sees as a medical practitioner. From that perspective, George is very different as a doctor. Many doctors treat the symptoms of their patients and send them on their way with enough medicine to dull their emotions. George spends quality time with patients, getting to know them and treating them from a holistic perspective. Most patients walk out of his office on their way to healing because they have found that place of love in their hearts, as someone has taken the time to listen and attempted to address the core issues.

Even though written from a Christian perspective, because George was raised Greek Orthodox and lives in a largely Christian community, the book expands into all religions, because all religions have a principle of love upon which their religious foundations are built, regardless of what naming they ascribe to that reality. As George has successfully reached many folks of all religious backgrounds in lunches and personal conversations, he does so here in a written fashion. In reading this book, I do caution you not to read it as a textbook, novel, or a quick read. It is meant to be read in a quiet, reflective mode and can be referred to many times depending upon one's state and place in life.

As you go forth into the book, know that love is the root and foundation of our lives, and perfect love will always cast out fear. Never be afraid to voice those longed-for words with a depth of meaning: "I love you!" George does that freely and encourages you to do likewise. As the Song of Songs says, "Hark my Lover, here he comes, leaping across mountains, bounding the hills." Love always finds a welcoming home in our hearts!

Father Steve Angi

ACKNOWLEDGMENTS

I would like to thank my wife, Raye Ann, who was kind enough to offer many invaluable suggestions as she read through multiple revisions of the manuscript from 2002 until 2007.

I would also like to thank Sue Vonderhaar, an editor at the *Cincinnati Enquirer*, whose efforts from the spring of 2007 until the summer of 2008 helped guide this book and its companion guide to a higher level. Sue, I very much appreciate your dedication to excellence as well as your willingness to share your enchanting stories. I will always cherish the time we spent together editing stories in a state of heightened energy.

Over the next few years, I worked on the books in quiet solitude. During this time, I found my energy soaring as spirit guided me in the most wondrous fashion. And so, I offer my most heartfelt thanks to God for allowing me to have such an incredible experience.

In the early months of 2011, I established a close friendship with Larry Hughes, a retired elementary school music teacher. Larry, to whom I lightheartedly refer as "Master of Nuance" of the English language, helped me to achieve greater clarity in these writings as we worked on the books through the spring of that year. Larry, I am most grateful to you for your remarkable efforts and for your willingness to serve as a sounding board with the books' further progression.

During the next few years, I returned to working on the books in peaceful solitude. So, once again, I offer my thanks to God for the opportunity to focus on these writings in a setting of communion and quiet stillness—for his encouragement and his understanding of my need to strive for excellence in a world without limits.

Prior to submitting this book for publication, Jim Knippling, a dear friend and professor of English at the University of Cincinnati, kindly offered to read it. Thank you, Jim, for your wonderful suggestions and grammatical reminders (the old dangling modifier and restrictive relative clause). It always fills me with joy when a sentence is strengthened.

My heartfelt appreciation also goes out to Elizabeth Day for doing an excellent job with line editing. Elizabeth, you are a true professional.

I would like to thank all of the exceptional people at Archway Publishing—Mateo, Jessica, Emma, Karol, Randy—as well as the gifted design team. A special thanks to Kayla for doing a great job as my concierge and to Adalee for her helpful advice on the cover design.

I would also like to thank Akayla Floyd, Kait Vonderhaar, Jack Heekin, Lisa Massa, Alan Vonderhaar, and Rylan Hixon for their meaningful input.

I would like to extend my appreciation to the Hollenkamp and Frondorf families. It has been a blessing listening to your stories of Aubrey Rose. Your loving family has enabled me to feel Aubrey's beautiful spiritual presence.

I would also like to thank Father Steve Angi, who smiles and laughs with the love and peace of God. Steve, I very much appreciate your friendship and your spiritual awareness.

I would like to extend a special thanks to my children, Suzanne and David, for helping me to understand and appreciate the mystical and limitless world in which we live. Your love, faith, and support have been tremendous. I can't begin to tell you how much you have enriched my life.

Lastly, I would like to thank my family (especially my mom, who has been absolutely wonderful), my friends, and my patients who have been extremely helpful and supportive. You have given me more gifts than I could ever imagine.

INTRODUCTION

Spirituality transcends religion
It arises from the heart
Enhancing, elevating, enriching

Dear Reader,

This book is an invitation. It is an opportunity for my son and me to explore and share our spiritual truths with you while inviting you to explore and share your truths with us. The stories in the book are all based on true life experiences, providing an opportunity for you to experience the truths of others as well. By identifying, embracing, and living our truths, we come to follow our own "path to peace" … we come to lead richer more fulfilled lives.

It is my hope that this book will help people discover the power within themselves, their intimate connection with the light of love, and the peace of their eternal spirit.

Since I live in a predominantly Christian community, many of the stories in this book are based on experiences from that perspective; however, I believe spirituality transcends religion, that it stems from the heart rather than the mind—enhancing, elevating, and enriching one's religious or nonreligious beliefs and experiences. Had my location been different, these stories could just as easily have been based on experiences from the perspective of any religious (Muslim, Jewish, Buddhist, Hindu, etc.) or nonreligious belief system. They are simply an expression of the universal language of love. Regardless of our religious affiliations or lack thereof, each of us has a meaningful story to tell. Each of us is a part of the beauty of the universe, a part of love.

George Sifri

Our journey with God
Inspires us to reflect upon our underlying beauty
Our essence of love

When we fully surrender
We fully awaken

When we fully awaken
We fully create

PROLOGUE

As dusk began to give way to darkness, David and I had to make a decision. We were stranded on a narrow ledge and needed to determine whether we would spend the night on the mountain or try to climb down. We knew we couldn't get back the way we came, and there were no clear alternatives.

We had come up the mountainside to achieve something greater, to begin a journey into the unknown. We felt the need to ask for guidance and to understand how to achieve the impossible—to break the barrier that existed between heaven and earth.

We sought to fully surrender, to fully awaken to the light of God—to experience oneness with all, love with all, on earth as it is in heaven.

After only a moment's consideration, we decided to stay on the mountainside. Months later I would discover that David, my four-teen-year-old son, would have been more than happy to head down the mountain that night and climb into his warm bed, but he said nothing. When I suggested we stay, he quickly assented. He had absolute faith in me ... and in God.

By then it was getting colder, and the winds were picking up. David's shorts were paper thin, and he was starting to shiver. I suggested he wear my sweater as pants—both arms of the sweater stretching over his legs, the body of it covering his waist. Although he was reluctant to take the sweater, he finally acquiesced. I was relieved. It was much easier for me to deal with the cold than to watch my son shivering.

After a while, we decided to lie down and get some sleep. As we lay on the rocks, using pinecones for pillows, the temperature dropped, and the wind picked up. Swarms of biting ants, nearly an inch in length, began to crawl on us. For the next several hours, we were overrun by these six-legged creatures as they wandered up our legs, under our shorts, and across our arms. We were pulling one off of us every thirty seconds. There was no stopping them.

Several hours later, they retreated. By that time, it was bitter cold, and the winds were howling. I didn't stop shivering for the rest of the night.

Around three in the morning, by my internal clock, I asked David if perhaps we might talk since neither of us was sleeping anyway. We began discussing inspirational books we had read, prayers we found to be especially meaningful, and our spiritual thoughts in general. For the next three hours, we shared these ideas and prayed together. I was feeling good. Even though it had been a difficult night, our faith remained strong as we turned to God during this challenging period. Although we didn't have a functioning clock, I knew it was approaching 6:00 a.m. It was time for the sun to rise.

I continued to watch for the morning light while reassuring David that it wouldn't be much longer, but the light didn't come. Instead of the dawn, we experienced only infinite blackness. Meanwhile the temperature continued to drop, and the winds became increasingly fierce. I couldn't understand what was going on. Where was the sun? Why wouldn't the dawn appear? As the minutes slowly ticked past, I began to get angry.

We had been guided by God to stay on this mountain. We had endured the dark, bitter-cold night with faith and prayer. We had traversed the course. Now, though, instead of crossing the finish line, we found ourselves freezing, exhausted, and confused in this no-man's land. The rules had changed. We were no longer experiencing time in the normal realm. Time had slowed to a crawl. While I awaited God's response to my questions, I felt nothing—no encouraging words, no comforting signs—only emptiness.

For the first time in my life, I began to accuse God of being insensitive, of leading us down a path and then abandoning us. Where was his gentleness? Where was his compassion?

As I reflected on the events of the night, it occurred to me that perhaps it wasn't God who had guided us on this path. Perhaps it was some other power, some negative-energy source. What the hell was going on?

Until now I had always been the one with the answers, with undying faith, the person others came to when life proved too difficult, when they had given up hope … but now it was I who was in despair. I found myself questioning my beliefs, questioning God. As the night wore on, time hung lifeless in the void. I was miserable, trapped in a disturbing dream, robbed of the promise of morning light.

The darkness seemed to continue forever. I sat there freezing in a T-shirt and shorts, surrounded by a vast emptiness filled only with silence. As I shook uncontrollably for hours on end, I found myself abandoning all hope.

PART I

It All Begins with Awareness

A quiet peace
An inner stillness
A soft awakening
To the light of love

CHAPTER 1

Can We Be Spiritual and Not Know It?

Warren, a patient of mine, came to see me for a physical on an annual basis. He always had a positive outlook and exuded vitality. He was seventy years old and frequently toured the country on his motorcycle visiting different state parks. Warren generally traveled by himself but met an array of people with whom he developed great friendships.

I enjoyed talking with Warren. He was the type of person who left you feeling energized.

Because his demeanor was so warm and inviting, I asked Warren one day whether he ever felt a strong connection with God or some higher source—especially during his travels to such beautiful parks. Taking little time to consider the question, he replied, "No."

His answer caught me off guard. I had never considered the possibility that Warren didn't consider himself to be either religious or spiritual. On reflection, I realized that I had attributed his sense of peace as emanating from a higher source, but that is not how he chose to view it.

We have all met people who exude exceptional warmth and

kindness but who claim to feel no real spiritual connection. In the end, it doesn't seem to matter what terms or labels we use. What appears to be most important is our ability to express that amazing quality of love that reflects who we truly are.

Like Warren, Susan never considered herself to be a spiritual person. She had always found peace in church settings and was moved by hymns and the spirit of Christmas. When asked about her spiritual beliefs, however, she would say she simply couldn't believe in something she couldn't see or that couldn't be proven scientifically.

One year while visiting Seattle, her hometown, Susan spent an afternoon hiking on the lower slopes of Mount Rainier, her favorite place in the world. As a kid playing in the backyard, she would look at that majestic peak rising in the distance and think, *Someday, I'm gonna stand on top of that mountain!* But as the years passed, and she eventually married and moved out of state, Susan never got around to it.

On that day, though, as she stood in the shadow of historic Paradise Inn, she watched with envy as groups of climbers clumped past her in their mountaineering gear, bound for the 14,411-foot summit. Reflecting on her dream, she turned to her brother and exclaimed, "We have to do this next year! It's now or never!" Shortly thereafter, they each launched into a yearlong training regimen to prepare for their two-day summit attempt.

When the big day finally arrived, Susan and her brother joined the climbing party outside the lodge where they nervously awaited their guides. After introducing themselves and checking and adjusting their equipment, they were off on their great adventure, but it didn't take long for them to realize how grueling the climb would be. It was with great relief that they finally reached the 11,500-foot level, where they slept just a few hours, then set out for the summit in the dead of night—before the sun could open crevasses in the softened snow.

"Staggering out of my sleeping bag at midnight on my stiff, aching legs," Susan said, "I stood there on that dark, quiet mountainside with the other climbers, eerily illuminated by each others' headlamps, and strapped on my heavy pack. I was so eager to tackle the top of that mountain. After trudging just a few hundred yards up the slope, I attempted to leap over a narrow crevasse in the snow, but my feet never left the ground. My tired legs had turned to jelly! My heart sank as I realized there was no summit in my future. This was as far as I was gonna go."

As the others continued on toward the summit, Susan wished her brother luck and hunkered down in the snow to wait for their return. At first she was furious with herself. Although she'd trained hard for a year, she had flown in from Ohio just two days earlier and understood now she should have acclimated to the altitude for a few days before trying to climb. When she finally stopped berating herself, she looked around and realized how incredibly quiet it was on that slope. All of a sudden, sitting there by herself in the dark, she became frightened. Here she was on the side of a mountain, at 2:00 a.m., completely alone. "Not a living thing anywhere. Not a sound. Just snow." She felt as if she were on the moon or another planet. She looked way down to the valley below and saw two tiny lights twinkling at the 5,000-foot level, the lodge where her husband slept. *How am I ever going to get down?* Susan wondered.

At that moment, she was seized by an absolutely irrational panic. "The kind of panic," Susan said, "an astronaut might experience on realizing he was stranded in space. I sat shivering in the snow, the stillness disturbed only by the pounding of my heart."

Gradually reason returned, and she thought to herself, *What are you worried about, you doofus? You'll just walk down in the morning!* Finally, after the moment of panic subsided, Susan started to relax.

"My pulse began to slow," she explained, "and I could feel the warm vapor of my breath inside the hood of my down parka. I gradually became aware of the whisper of a light wind, and I was greatly comforted by the deep blue-black sky. Sitting there on my perch, high above the earth, I felt a calm settle over me unlike any I had ever experienced. I was suddenly at one with the stars, the moon, the mountain, the trees below—the entire universe—and as I retreated into that long, timeless moment, my mind quieted, my heart filled with love, and I knew I wasn't alone."

Religion teaches us we should love
Spirituality teaches us we are love

CHAPTER 2

What Is Spirituality?

I think people in general assume spirituality and religion are one and the same, but I view them as separate. Religion is based on an individual accepting and following the principles, beliefs, and doctrines of a particular faith, whereas spirituality arises from a person's heart and is unique to each individual.

Being spiritual may be defined as *feeling* a connection with some energy, being, or force that is greater than ourselves, but even this definition may be too narrow. A broader definition might be *feeling* connected, at least intermittently, with a sense of love or peace.

Spirituality is so rich, so multifaceted, that to try to limit our understanding of it to a sharply focused black-and-white picture diminishes our experience. Sometimes it is better to simply ask questions than to seek answers. For example, one might ask oneself ...

Who am I?

I remember watching the actor Al Pacino being interviewed on the Bravo network. I was intrigued by his answer when he was asked how he develops his characters. He said that as he reads through a script, he will jot down questions about his character in the margins, but he doesn't really try to answer the questions. Instead, he leaves them open and stays receptive to ideas or details that will strengthen his character over time.

We can all benefit by adopting a similar approach toward

spirituality. If we leave the door open for evolving thoughts and new information rather than concrete answers, we end up with a much more meaningful experience.

Imagine, for instance, that you are standing under a waterfall. The water flowing over you is the essence of spirituality. As you cup your hands in an attempt to capture the spiritual essence, you're able to hold on to very little. If, on the other hand, you allow the water to wash over you as you focus on the taste, touch, smell and sensation of the water, your experience is much richer. Rather than trying to contain the spiritual experience within a small area and thereby limit it, you become immersed in it. Your appreciation is all the grander because you have had the opportunity to commune with the water—to feel God's presence. You have come to understand that the essence of spirituality is something much greater than yourself and you are left feeling humbled.

ॐ

One day while talking to one of my patients, Kristin, about spirituality, we began to talk about an interesting shamanic belief that each of us has an animal with whom we can closely identify. This "spirit animal" has meaningful characteristics that remind us of our strengths and help us to better understand our individual approaches to life. When Kristin asked me what my animal was, I told her I felt a close connection with the turtle.

In mythology, the rounded shell of the turtle is thought to represent heaven, and its flat lower shell, the earth. The turtle, then, is thought to be a bridge between heaven and earth. Humans who identify with the turtle may likewise serve as a link between heaven and earth. They may find themselves immersed in the realm of spirituality as they encourage others to share their spiritual thoughts and experiences. Some additional qualities of the turtle include its slow-moving disposition (the turtle seldom rushes; it's in the moment), its perseverance, and its strength.

Kristin, an animal lover, had never heard of spirit animals and was intrigued. After asking a few questions about how one might identify one's spirit animal, she said, "It sounds weird, but I've always shared a special affinity for the salmon. Not the kind of affinity I have for dogs and birds but some kind of indescribable bond."

She went on to tell me that she had always felt a powerful pull to the far, far north and had enjoyed trips to Scandinavia, Iceland, and northern Canada. She said she'd long been fascinated by Eskimos and the spiritual relationships they share with animals. Whenever she buys anything Eskimo-related—art, jewelry, wall hangings—she finds herself gravitating toward the Eskimo salmon symbol.

"I had never really thought about that until you mentioned your turtle," she said, and then she shared a story with me.

About two years ago while on an Alaskan cruise with her family, Kristin decided to climb a mountain that towered over the docks in Skagway where the cruise ship was moored for the day. It was her birthday, and for some reason all she wanted to do was go hiking by herself.

"I started my hike in the early afternoon," Kristin said, "as other hikers were coming down the trail, and I felt as if I had the whole mountain to myself. It was a brilliant August day and incredibly peaceful in those lush northern woods. As I walked along the trail that circled the base of the steep mountainside, I came upon a fast-running stream that was alive with activity. At first, I thought the motion was just water rushing over the rocks, but then I looked more closely into the roiling water and realized it was full of salmon. The bright-red fish were fighting their way through the shallow water toward the quiet pool upstream where they would spawn. As I stood at the edge of the stream and watched the exhausted, bloodied fish, scarred by their long battle up the river, leaping waterfalls and slamming into rocks, I felt a rush of admiration for the instinct that drives them to such extremes.

"The water was only about one or two feet deep," she continued, "and there must have been hundreds of salmon thrashing about. I stood there for the longest time watching those salmon. I hated to leave. I felt such a powerful bond with those fish."

Intrigued by the idea of the salmon as a spirit animal after our talk, Kristin did some reading about the symbolism of salmon in folklore. "In many cultures," she explained, "the salmon represents wisdom, perseverance, and determination in its quest for spiritual truths. The salmon swims upstream, fighting its daily battles—leaping obstacles, butting boulders—but continually forging ahead to its destiny ... to reunite with the divine. It is always journeying home, instinctively trusting in the unknown, often struggling, but gaining insight along the way."

Recalling the inexplicable bond she'd shared with those fish while standing at that river's edge, Kristin realized now that those strong feelings had been spiritual in nature, and she took great comfort in that.

"I was no longer one lone individual walking through life with no defined purpose. Instead, I felt that I was one of many, forging ahead on a much bigger journey ... toward a much grander destiny."

Following her visit, Kristin sent me a note of appreciation. While expressing her gratitude for our shared experience, she went on to tell me she had gained some further insight into her spirit animal.

"I sometimes think of my salmon and its inclination to butt its head against boulders and keep slamming its body into the waves as it moves forward, sometimes bullheadedly, sometimes even recklessly," she wrote. "And during difficult or stressful times, when I do consciously think of that personality 'type' and admit how I am, and why, I'm better able to tell myself to slow down, to find a quiet eddy in the stream and meditate in the clear water of that pool and get my bearings before continuing on. I'm better able to remind myself that we are all on the same path, searching for the same things, but each animal goes about it differently. It helps me to be aware of those differences and appreciate the beauty in each animal, but most of all my little salmon."

☙

If I sense that my patients are open to the subject, I often talk to them about spirituality because it can be such a potent healer. I suggest they connect with *their* spirituality as much as possible in whatever manner works for them.

I, personally, have found listening to music, reading, walking, meditation, nature, and writing to be powerful connectors. I also feel energized when I am exchanging spiritual ideas and experiences with others in a setting of shared intimacy. In such situations, I often find myself in a state of pure joy as I bask in the heightened energy of love.

☙

Jenny came to see me one day with an upper-respiratory infection. As we talked, I discovered she was studying hard to get into graduate school. She felt that medicine was her true calling but had not applied to medical school, fearing that she would not be accepted even though her grades were quite good.

It became apparent during our talk that Jenny had felt a strong spiritual connection in past years. Over time, however, she had lost touch with those feelings. Fear had overtaken love. She possessed many strengths that would make her a great physician, but somewhere along the line, she had forgotten her passion. She was going through the motions of life without much joy or sense of purpose.

As we discussed spirituality, her life's path, and the possibilities that lay before her, I could sense an increasingly energized atmosphere. Jenny's eyes brightened, and she began talking with unbridled enthusiasm about previous spiritual experiences—signs and events in her life that had elicited feelings of communion and empowerment, of love and appreciation.

One of those powerful experiences was horseback riding. Jenny recalled how she would enter the stable and immediately feel comforted by the familiar smell of hay and manure, the muted sounds of animals stirring, the slowing of time. As she stroked her horse and focused her attention on the coarseness of his hair, the warmth of his body, she would cease to worry. Looking into his big brown eyes, her mind would go adrift ... until the sound of his snorting startled her, reminding her that it was time to ride, to be free.

They would start out slowly, at a trot. Gradually her horse would shift into a canter and, finally, into a graceful gallop. As he accelerated further, like a racehorse in full stride, she would lean in close and become aware of the wetness around his neck, the matting of his short hair, the flaring of his nostrils—sharing a oneness of spirit with the magnificent creature beneath her. There was a release of control as her legs gripped his tense body tightly and securely. With heightened energy, the cool air rushing over her, she found herself gliding effortlessly, surrendering totally.

As Jenny described her ride, she transformed into a much more impassioned and vibrant person—one who appeared to be a thousand miles away, in a place devoid of fear and enveloped in beauty.

I do not know whether Jenny continued on to medical school, nor do I know whether she continued to feed her spiritual nature. I do know that when she left my office she was soaring with truth and light, with clarity of purpose and hope, with the joyful remembrance of who she was.

CHAPTER 3

Spirituality Is a Feeling

I like to ask about the spirituality of patients who are depressed or stressed, since it can be a very helpful tool. The response I get most often is, "Well, I don't go to church regularly." I then explain that I am not asking about church. I'm asking whether they *feel* a connection with something greater than themselves. Perhaps they might define this as God or some other positive energy force. Invariably at this point, many patients say they do consider themselves to be spiritual.

❧

A patient of mine, Lauren, came to see me for a physical. Lauren intrigued me. Despite having four children and a husband who traveled frequently, she was happily raising her family, paying the bills, and doing all the housework. She said she loved to work, and she loved to keep busy. In fact, her most difficult challenge was trying to sit still on vacations. Lauren's parents had a similar ethic. Her father was retired but stayed active with multiple projects, as did her mother.

While we talked, and I addressed Lauren's medical questions, I became curious as to whether spirituality played a role in her life—a life that appeared centered and positive, one that she embraced. In response, Lauren told me that she was uncertain of the existence of God. If God did exist, however, she was sure that nature, which brought her great peace and comfort, was an integral part of God's spirit.

During our conversation, I discovered that Lauren had lost a son several years earlier. Her child had been whisked from her arms shortly after his birth. For the next two months, he was in a neonatal intensive-care unit connected by a maze of wires to a multitude of monitors. Whenever Lauren went to pick him up, the monitors would go off, preventing her from holding him for any period of time. Lauren recalled that her son had looked his best when he was first delivered, as she held him close to her breast for forty-five minutes free of the entangling equipment.

She told me that, oddly enough, the most comforting part of the whole experience was when she was once again able to quietly hold her baby boy as he was dying—to lovingly and tenderly experience the mother-son bond. While we talked, tears began to stream down her cheeks. They were silent, free-flowing tears that spoke of hardship and pain, of a mother's undying love. Lauren felt embarrassed—crying was only to be done in private. Besides, she had four other healthy children. Shouldn't she be focusing on the positives?

As I watched Lauren, I felt great appreciation for the wonderful bond that obviously still existed between her and her son. From my perspective, it was simply beautiful, yet her uncertainty regarding a spiritual universe left her full of questions. *What if there was no God? What if there was no heaven? What if her baby ended up in heaven and she didn't?*

Lauren's husband was religious. He and their children attended a Catholic church regularly. Lauren, however, had reservations about Catholicism. In her view, her husband's religion didn't embrace nature as an integral part of spirit, and this bothered her. She remained uncertain of the existence of God and whether her perception of God fit within traditional Christian thought. Yet when she lost her son, she received an outpouring of love and sympathy from her husband's congregation, and it touched her deeply, causing her to feel that the congregation was connected with spirit, that they were on a good path. Lauren was left feeling lost as to what to believe. How was she to know the truth about God, about religion, about spiritual happenings, about the possibility of life after death?

I asked Lauren whether she had ever experienced any communication from her son. She said that she had driven by a park recently and noticed a child playing—a child whose age would have been the same as her little boy's had he lived. After reflecting on what her own son might have been like at that age, she looked up and saw a street sign with his name on it. She felt touched and wondered if, on some level, he was communicating with her. She went on to tell me that these coincidences happened all the time but that she was hesitant to interpret them as anything more than wishful thinking.

I decided to tell Lauren a story that I hoped might encourage her to trust her intuition and experiences. It was a story about one of my patients, a sixty-year-old vivacious nun named Shirley.

One year previously, when Shirley was driving to her swim club, she impulsively decided to turn in the direction opposite from her club. Shirley would often get feelings urging her to follow a different path from the one initially intended, and she was quick to acquiesce. She continued driving, making a series of turns based on her intuition, and ended up at a building owned by her order.

She walked over to it and cautiously opened the door, at which point she was invited in by the facilitator.

"We've been waiting for you," he said, catching her by surprise.

He then told her they were about to begin a guided meditation session during which the participants would come to know the animal with whom they were most intimately connected. This was based on the shamanic belief that each person has positive traits that closely mimic those of a particular animal—a power animal—that might help them on their life journey, similar to Kristin's salmon in chapter 2. The facilitator went on to explain that they would initially see a solitary animal but that this would soon be followed by a visualization of a large number of such animals.

Shirley had always felt drawn to butterflies and was expecting to visualize one as her animal. As she began her meditation, she wasn't surprised to find herself walking through a forest, its lush vegetation providing the perfect butterfly setting.

She soon approached a clearing that was wet and muddy. Shirley attempted to walk around the swampy area but suddenly felt herself descend into its depths. She let out a tiny shriek as she was literally taken into the earth and swallowed up whole. At the next moment, however, Shirley emerged on the other side, surprised to find herself unscathed and unsoiled, walking on a beach. When she looked around at her new surroundings and saw no signs of trees or bushes, she was perplexed. How was she to locate her butterflies?

As Shirley turned her attention toward the ocean, something startled her.

"Oh my God!" she exclaimed.

Shirley found herself face to face with a huge bluish-grey dolphin whose head was over two feet wide and who was looking straight at her. Although the dolphin was far out in the water, it seemed so close. It appeared to be smiling at her with eyes that held her attention, eyes that pierced her soul. She was captivated by its magnificence, but it wasn't a butterfly. She didn't understand. Where were her butterflies?

Shirley remembered the facilitator had told her that after she first saw her animal, she would visualize many more of them. Since this hadn't happened, perhaps the dolphin wasn't her animal after all. Then as she looked back at the ocean, she was stunned by the appearance of hundreds of dolphins, leaping over the surf, in and out of the water, staring at her—their light blue color contrasting with the whiteness of the waves. She stood watching, mesmerized. She could hardly breathe as her heart filled with love for these gentle creatures.

When she came out of the guided meditation, Shirley still wasn't certain what to believe. Was this visualization just a dream? She sat uncharacteristically quiet as she listened to the others tell their stories. She thought she could escape without speaking. Finally, the facilitator and the rest of the class asked her to share her experience. Although she was reluctant, she was told that they already knew much of her story from the sounds she had been emitting throughout her mediation; they just wanted her to fill in the details.

☙

I asked Shirley how the meditative experience had affected her. What was the significance of the animals? She told me she now realized that animals and nature are as much a part of the beauty and majesty of God as we are; we are all part of the whole. We are all interconnected; there is no artificial separation, no artificial hierarchy.

I felt there was also another message in the story, however—one that has to do with our reluctance to trust our own experiences when they do not fit into a set of previously held beliefs. We continue to search for butterflies when dolphins are in front of us; we are hesitant to embrace experiences that seem unreal yet which bring us great joy, such as signs from a deceased, loving son.

☙

As I finished telling Lauren this story, she eagerly told me that, like Shirley, she frequently took unusual paths while driving. She would sometimes take a different route to a destination, even if it was longer or more circuitous, based on a feeling. When I asked her whether her intuition had proven to be right in these matters, she told me she wasn't sure because she didn't know what would have happened had she taken her usual route; yet Lauren continued to follow her intuition as she was driving—trusting feelings that she could neither see, hear, nor touch.

I asked Lauren how she had felt in the past when she encountered the "signs" from her deceased son. She told me she wondered if she was just imagining them. I tried to clarify my question. I didn't want to know about her thoughts; I wanted to know about her feelings.

"What did you feel in your heart when you saw those signs?" I asked.

"I felt my son was communicating with me," she answered through quiet unrelenting tears. "My heart came alive with love."

I went on to express my feeling that our individual truths—our sacred beliefs—always lie within our hearts, that it is the mind that creates the problems and doubts. I then shared some of my patients' experiences with post-death communication.

Eventually, Lauren's husband called her to ask her where she was. He was speechless when he discovered that she had been crying in front of me. This was not the Lauren he knew.

As she left my office, Lauren gave me a big hug and thanked me. She knew her son had been communicating with her. Her heart had called out to him, and he had responded with signs of love to remind her that life and love are eternal ... that there was nothing to fear ... that he would always be with her.

There are as many religions
As there are individuals

—Mahatma Gandhi

CHAPTER 4

We Need to Find Our Own Spiritual Path

Norm's demeanor spoke of gentleness and humility in spite of his many academic accomplishments. His smile was easy and his eyes kind. He had been diagnosed with cancer a few years previously and was now beginning experimental treatments for his illness.

During our conversation, I discovered that Norm, who was Jewish, was not particularly religious. As a matter of fact, he did not believe in God, but he had come to appreciate the Eastern approach to life, specifically the practice of meditation.

At different times throughout his day, Norm would go into a meditative state. His breathing would slow, and his mind would grow quiet. He would become the "watcher"—at one with the moment. In this detached manner, he would no longer attempt to control the world around him but simply allow. His anxieties would melt away as he entered a place of peace.

Norm told me that he and his wife recently traveled to California to visit their son, who had some health issues and was not taking care of himself. While there, some heated family discussions took place regarding their son's condition. In the course of these conversations, Norm could feel his anxiety rising. At such times, he would shift into a meditative state. His mind would become still as he concentrated on his breathing … slow breath in, slow breath out. He could feel the tension slipping away. A feeling of tranquility would envelop him as he listened to the conversation in a more detached manner—as an observer with heightened awareness.

After describing his experiences with meditation, Norm began asking me about my spiritual beliefs. As an atheist, he was curious as to why I believed in the existence of God. I told him that when I was spiritually connected, I couldn't help but feel the presence of God. During such times, I felt an intense love for everything around me; all fear disappeared. It was this feeling of love that inspired my faith. As I spoke of this wonderful feeling, Norm looked at me and said, "Yes, that feeling that you are describing, that's what I am talking about. That's the feeling I get when I meditate."

I was stunned to discover that Norm and I were experiencing the same feeling—love without boundaries. I termed this love *God;* he termed it *peace*. My world was spiritual, and his was not, but our experiences were one and the same. It was only the labels that separated us.

ॐ

Light leads
And love follows

—*Mitchell Kleinholz*

He stood four foot six with dark brown hair and freckles. His name was Mitchell, and he was not your typical nine-year-old boy. After talking with his mother and hearing about his strong connection with love and spirit, I invited him to breakfast. He came with a list of things *he* wanted to talk about.

As he sat opposite me in the restaurant booth, I leaned back and listened. It was easy to see that Mitchell was full of love. His voice was soft and his demeanor reflective. He was quick to offer a warm smile and a shy laugh.

Mitchell began talking about nature—about how it is a gift from spirit. He compared it to a great amusement park: open to everyone, easily accessible, and abundantly beautiful.

Mitchell talked next of love and karma—about how the kindnesses we extend to others come back to us magnified. As he spoke, a waitress walked by. She smiled at me and gently touched my shoulder. Mitchell looked up at me and said this was an example of karma. He went on to say that I had helped this waitress, and now she was sending me love. I found this quite interesting. Unbeknownst to him, I had been helping her with some challenges her daughter was facing, yet I hadn't shared this information with Mitchell. I couldn't help but wonder how he could be so intuitive.

As we continued to talk, Mitchell traced his small finger across the table and said that we all have a path to walk. We can bypass the obstacles we encounter if we desire, but the purpose of our existence is to face these challenges. He focused on the plastic cup in front of him and said that each challenge is like a cup—that is, like a hill. Although the hill might be steep at times, once we get to the top, we can enjoy the feeling of having scaled the hill as well as the thrill of the downhill slide.

After he said this, I noticed a distant look in his eye—as if he were connecting with something higher. Mitchell went on to say that the front of the hill was bumpy, whereas the back of the hill was slick, like oil. If we climb the hill and stop part of the way up, the slide back down the front of the hill is uncomfortable. It is rough and slow in contrast to the ride down the back of the hill, which is smooth and fast. He further said that there are exit points on the hill, where people can take different paths as they climb, paths that are somewhat easier, paths that are "good enough," but then sliding down the back of the hill isn't as fun. It's incomplete. By taking an alternate route, climbers limit their experience. It is best to go all the way up the hill.

Mitchell then stated that the more we resist the challenges in our lives, the more difficult they will become. He used the boomerang as an analogy, "the harder you throw it, the more forcefully it returns."

I asked him, "Will our challenges ever end?"

"No," he said. "We will always have challenges.

"What will change, however, is the way we choose to deal with them. With time we will learn to embrace those challenges. This will make all the difference."

Later, I asked Mitchell what he thought Jesus had come to teach us. Mitchell reminded me that Jesus had challenged the conventional theological dogma of the day by questioning widely accepted religious practices. Jesus taught us that we should be free to follow our own beliefs, just as he espoused a new doctrine of spiritual love.

Mitchell emphasized that our differences are our common ground. Our differences make each of us unique and therefore alike. He recalled the inspirational words of the Rev. Martin Luther King Jr. that spoke of the right of all individuals to pursue their dreams, that spoke of celebrating our individual differences as well as our similarities. Mitchell summarized his own thoughts by saying, "We should be free to have our own beliefs while remembering that the thoughts of others are higher than our own."

ॐ

I remember offering a ceramic bluish-green cross to a waitress named Adina at a restaurant several years ago. It was the holiday season, and I was there with my then-sixteen-year-old daughter, Suzanne. Adina was wonderfully attentive to our needs, and I intuitively offered her the handmade cross as a gift. As she unwrapped the present, a smile spread across her face. At the time, I was unaware that Adina was Jewish, but that had no effect on the heartfelt appreciation she showed for the gift—or on her understanding of the love that accompanied it. As we talked, I came to discover that Adina often visited different churches in an effort to broaden her spirituality.

I love crosses—all shapes, sizes, and colors—especially crosses handmade from unique materials. I love to give crosses to people, whether they are Christian or not. It makes no difference to me. In my mind, a cross speaks the universal language of love, the ever-present beauty of spirit.

My love of crosses reflects my love of Christ whose presence I feel so strongly, so intimately. It is not a presence that speaks of boundaries but one that speaks of invitation—of opportunities—of a hand extended with love and light. When I offer a cross, I am offering an intimate part of myself, an intimate part of God. I offer this not to persuade or convert but to comfort and touch.

ॐ

One fall day I was leaving a Catholic bookstore with a newly purchased cross. It was eight inches tall and made of a richly finished wood. A golden figure of Jesus was attached to it, a look of serenity on his face—his arms, no longer affixed to the cross, outstretched in invitation. It was a welcoming cross, one that spoke of love and surrender.

Upon getting into my car to leave the bookstore, I had a feeling I should wait. Inside the shop, I had noticed a woman standing in line behind me. I sensed the cross was meant for her.

I busied myself in my car for a while, but she remained inside the store. I finally decided to give it five more minutes; if it was meant to happen, she would appear. A short time later, she left the shop. I got out of my car and walked toward her.

As I approached her, I looked into her eyes and handed her the box. "I have a feeling I should give this to you," I said. "I don't know why."

Her eyes widened with surprise as she reluctantly took the gift. "This isn't necessary," she responded.

She slowly opened the box. After noticing what lay inside, tears began to stream down her face.

As she delicately fingered the cross, she said, "My brother just died yesterday, and I have been struggling ever since. This morning I asked God for a sign to let me know he was fine."

Her tears continued to flow as she gave me a hug and extended a soft-spoken thank you.

Upon walking away, I thought to myself...

He does work in mysterious ways but always, always, with love.

In the setting of appreciation
Noise fades
And love abounds

CHAPTER 5

We Foster Spirituality through Appreciation

When we choose to explore our spirituality, we often do not know how or where to begin. Our lives are full of noise. We desire to feel peace but are uncertain of how to achieve it. We crave silence, beauty, and oneness of spirit.

No matter what our spiritual or religious beliefs, we can begin by giving thanks—offering appreciation for the many blessings that have been bestowed upon us.

☙

Mana was in her early twenties, with long brown hair, a curvaceous figure, and a quick smile. She was one of those college-aged girls who always looked as if she had just stepped out of a shower, fresh and vibrant. Much like a sixties child, she was searching for her spiritual truths in a nontraditional fashion. Often drifting like the wind, she would work odd jobs and travel as her money allowed.

Mana's bohemian lifestyle afforded her the opportunity to study both North and South American Indian cultures. Through her explorations, she had developed a wonderful appreciation of nature. As she walked barefoot through the woods, her senses would heighten. Mana would listen closely to the musical sounds of the birds, feel the soft and uneven surface of the soil beneath her feet, and smell the fragrance of pine in the air. She would notice the cool breeze caressing her skin, the quiet motion of the surrounding plants and foliage. She would experience the roughness of the tree bark, the softness of the long grass, the waxy texture of the leaves.

Through it all, Mana would give thanks. She would offer gratitude to the water as it flowed beneath her, the wind as it stirred the grasses and trees, the sun as it warmed her back. She could feel the energy within the forest, and it spoke to her.

Venturing through the woods, she was one with all.

❦

Jeffrey was an executive for the auto industry. He was raised as a Catholic and always felt a strong connection with his faith, but at times he found his beliefs—his truths—weren't enough. Although he adhered to the principles of his religion, he felt he had lost sight of something greater. He recognized that without flexibility, *without love,* those sacred values and beliefs could break and shatter like the rigid branches of an aging tree in the midst of a violent storm.

Over the past year, Jeffrey had become frustrated and disillusioned with his job. His boss showed little appreciation for his talents and work ethic, and the auto industry was under a lot of financial pressure. For months Jeffrey had prayed for a new job to become available, but he felt his prayers were not being answered. He was approaching fifty and knew his chances of obtaining favorable employment elsewhere were slim. During this time, he grew irritable and depressed, uncertain of where to turn. He became increasingly angry with God and eventually lost faith that his prayers would ever be answered.

Jeffrey finally decided to try a different approach. Although he had been praying for a year without the desired results, he would now pray with love instead of fear. He would focus on substance over form. It was one thing to go to church weekly as evidence of his faith;

it was quite another to surrender himself to God, to ask for help and humble himself.

For two weeks, Jeffrey attended Mass daily. As he did so, he began to feel a quiet reassurance. He was communing with God in a way that brought back familiar feelings of hope and empowerment. In the past, his religion had always been a source of strength and enlightenment, but of late his prayers had become empty appeals lacking intimacy and passion. Now, however, his prayers were rich with love and embracing of guidance; they invited beauty and light into his heart. Jeffrey once again felt at peace with himself and with God.

Following this two-week period, a friend called Jeffrey out of the blue with an exciting job prospect. When the subject of salary arose during his initial interview, Jeffrey smiled and lightheartedly told the interviewer, "I am too old to play games; this is the salary I need."

The woman, who was in her early sixties, smiled back at him, and playfully said, "I, too, am too old for games. Just ask the next interviewer for three thousand dollars more than you want, and you'll get the salary you desire."

Within several days, Jeffrey landed the job of his dreams.

In time, Jeffrey came to realize that his prayers should center on worship—praise and thanksgiving. As he observed Muslims praying on their knees several times a day, he felt they had it right. They approached God differently. The practice of their faith highlighted the need for worship—the need to give God daily recognition as the Creator—as the Father. He remembered how his mother would pray with her prayer cards every morning in the kitchen. She had that same respect and love. Rather than asking for help, her focus was centered on giving thanks.

As Jeffrey continued on his spiritual path, he noticed changes in his personality. His emotions were closer to the surface. He could smile and laugh at the drop of a hat, and cry just as easily, without embarrassment. There was so much to appreciate.

One day Jeffrey told me about his eighteen-year-old son, Tyler, who was struggling with alcohol and drug dependency. Jeffrey described how he had tried to do everything possible to help Tyler—from convincing a college administrator that Tyler be allowed to retake an important entrance exam (one given without knowledge of his learning disability), to helping ensure that Tyler stay gainfully employed with someone who valued him. Jeffrey often told Tyler, "You may choose to give up on yourself, but I never will."

Jeffrey recalled a time when he had to physically intervene to keep Tyler from leaving the house to satisfy a drug craving. As Jeffrey's youngest son, Zach, walked into the kitchen and saw his father and big brother engaged in a heated scuffle, he started to cry. Jeffrey, who had his older son in a headlock, simply looked up at young Zach, smiled reassuringly, and asked, "What's wrong?"

Jeffrey's reaction reflected the love of a father trying to save one son from himself while simultaneously trying to ease the fears of the other.

As Jeffrey told me this story, tears of laughter filled his eyes. Life was absurd. Appearances no longer mattered. Despite how things looked, Jeffrey's physical clash with Tyler was an expression of love. It showed that beliefs and values can't exist in a vacuum; life has a way of tempering such seemingly absolute ideas.

In the past, it had always been important for Jeffrey to follow through with his ultimatums. He remembered telling Tyler one night, "If you go out with Ted, and you end up smoking pot, you can no longer stay in this house." Tyler did go out with Ted, and despite his initial intention not to smoke marijuana, he succumbed. In the old days, Jeffrey would have stayed true to his word, no matter the cost, but things were different now. Sticking to the rigid enforcement of his principles would only serve to distance himself from his son; there were other priorities.

Jeffrey knew that Tyler was a wonderful kid at heart. He was touched whenever Tyler expressed his appreciation for the faith his father had placed in him. He was moved when he witnessed Tyler's sensitivity to others—how, for instance, Tyler would always insist on sitting outside with the construction workers at lunch—the ones who worked under him—as he told stories in their native Italian and broke bread with them.

Jeffrey also knew that Tyler would continue to have his ups and downs. He related how he often stayed up late at night with Tyler when he was struggling, when he was tempted to turn to his old vices, and talk to him until he fell asleep. Together they would fight the good fight.

As Jeffrey shared these stories with me, he was smiling. He was amused with himself—understanding how much he had grown and realizing how much Tyler had taught him. He had come to recognize that all the religious values in the world, all those sacred beliefs, were nothing without gentleness.

Now he blessed each day, for he had come to appreciate the true beauty in his son and in life. It was love.

Of simple beauty
Quiet walks
And laughter

CHAPTER 6

Spirituality amid the Joy of Laughter

*I*t was Father's Day, and the kids were looking forward to our family attending church and having a nice lunch together. I had awakened at 7:00 a.m. while the rest of the family slept. I planned to go out for breakfast, write for a couple of hours, and then meet them for the service. My lower back was feeling tight, and by the time I left the house, it was giving me problems, but I made it to the restaurant without too much difficulty.

As I worked, the pain in my back gradually worsened. After an hour, I decided to return home, but when I tried to stand up, my legs felt wobbly. My backpack, which held my laptop, books, and papers, was relatively heavy, and as I left the restaurant, I wasn't sure I could make it to the parking lot without falling. I walked in a slumped-over position, trying to relieve some of the pressure on my back, and finally managed to get to the car but not without a number of curious stares and kind offers of help.

Once home, I realized there was little chance of my making it to church, much less to lunch. My wife told the kids, and I could sense their disappointment.

As I lay in bed trying to get comfortable, I had a thought: what better place to heal my back than in church, especially since I was finding it difficult to imagine my family attending a Father's Day service without me. I decided to take a hot bath and see if it would improve my situation. With a smile on my face, I told the kids, "God will heal me."

Once out of the bath, I felt somewhat better. After getting dressed with the help of my son, I managed to inch my way down to the car. We finally made it to church and sat in the near-empty balcony where I had the freedom to get up and walk around.

After the service, I left the church with some mild discomfort and proceeded to the restaurant. Given the uncertainty of my condition, I had decided to drive separately. The heated seat in my car relaxed my back, and my open convertible provided me with a pleasant distraction. It was a beautiful, sunny day, and I enjoyed listening to Amy Grant sing "Hymns for the Journey" as I drove along the Ohio River.

Within twenty minutes, I arrived at a seafood restaurant that sits at the edge of the Ohio River and offers a wonderful view of the Cincinnati skyline. Once we were seated, I thought it would be a good idea to get up every fifteen minutes and stretch. I didn't want to reexperience the stiffness I'd encountered that morning.

Our lunch was filled with lots of humor; I could tell that my wife and kids were happy that I was able to join them. At times, however, my back would spasm, and I would let out a shriek of pain, reacting to what felt like an electric jolt. At first, my convulsive movements caught my family off guard, but we quickly came to laugh at my spontaneous jerks—about how at any moment I might knock the food off the table, and about how my resolve to attend the lunch offered the other diners some interesting sights and sounds.

When I returned home, I decided to lie down and rest my back. Later that afternoon, I tried to stand up and get dressed, but I found even the slightest movement all but impossible. We had plans to go to my mother's house for a Father's Day dinner, but when I tried to walk down the stairs, I knew I was in serious trouble. A sharp pain going from my lower back down into my thighs forced me into a crouching position. The pain was so severe I literally couldn't breathe. I felt as if my back were going to break. I was frozen, unable to go either down the stairs or back up them. After several minutes, the pain finally subsided, and I managed to hobble back upstairs and get into my bed.

As I lay there, I began thinking about it being Father's Day and about missing my mother's dinner. My father had passed away almost two years before, and this was an important day to me for a number of reasons: my mother had gone to a lot of trouble preparing a nice meal; it could be a difficult day for her, given the recent death of my father; and we were planning to celebrate my son's birthday that night as well.

Once again, motivated by the power of spirit, I took another warm bath to see if it would ease the pain. To my surprise, after the bath I was able to dress myself—slowly. I then decided to catch up with the rest of my family at my mother's house. I was moving cautiously, but I was moving.

As I drove to Mom's house, I reflected on the last twelve hours. Although I had been in discomfort throughout the day, the pain was never prolonged; it would come and go. My focus, however, was not on the pain but rather on my family and the care they had extended to me. Most of the day was spent in laughter. I was the butt of many jokes, although even God took a little of the ribbing. Earlier in the day when I had supported myself by pushing a rolling chair toward the warm bath, I proclaimed that God had healed me in church. At the time, I was bent over and inching forward, obviously still in pain. When I laughed, my back would spasm, and I would almost drop to the floor. Although barely able to walk, I proclaimed the healing power of God and church with one arm raised, and the kids and I laughed almost to the point of tears.

But all joking aside, God really *had* healed me. He had healed me in the sense that I had been able to go to church with my family, to stroke my son's face and my daughter's hand as we listened to the service, and then to share a wonderful lunch afterwards. I was truly grateful.

Later that evening as I prepared to leave my mother's house, I gingerly eased out of my chair and onto the floor. My back was stiff, and I had to crawl about ten feet before painfully yet successfully being able to stand. With the help of a walker, I managed to shuffle out to my car.

I was thankful I had made it to my mother's dinner. Seeing all the smiling faces, eating the delicious food, and listening to all the amusing stories had filled my heart with joy. Everyone's spirits had been high, especially mine. I was so appreciative of having been afforded the opportunity to experience such a warm and lighthearted evening.

I was reminded of the difference between pain and suffering. Although I had endured pain that day, I had experienced very little suffering. It had been a great day—a day during which I had felt very close to God despite—or because of—my physical limitations. My awareness of the love that surrounded me, from both family and spirit, had left me feeling exhilarated.

Driving home, I came to realize something else—when we endure pain, God endures it as well. It is inconceivable that God could walk beside us and understand us intimately without also feeling our discomfort and our bliss. I suddenly understood how God could exist in a world that often lacked gentleness.

I had never fully comprehended this concept before. When we suffer at the hand of another, or by disease or through an act of nature, God is not sitting idly by. He is right there with us, experiencing the discomfort with us, walking with us every step of the way. Yet his faith in humanity and his respect for free will keep him from doing more. He can plant seeds of hope and create directional signs for us to see along our way, but in the end, God will be patiently waiting—knowing that love will prevail, knowing that we are all capable of creating miracles, knowing that with time will come understanding.

In the meantime, God will continue to walk with us, listen to us, and whisper sweetly of a wonderful place called love—a place that exists deep within our hearts and souls, amid kind smiles and joyful laughter.

A Prayer of Love, Affirmation, and Gratitude[1]

Oh heavenly Father of Light
Who graciously accompanies me on every walk
Who guides me with gentleness on the journey of life
Who reminds me of the joy of service and the power of simple truths
I humbly extend my love, appreciation, and gratitude

In you, I see only beauty, an outstretched hand, a tender touch
Through you, I live with a quiet mind, an open heart, an awareness of being
With you, I radiate a warm and inviting spiritual light
As I experience sweet whisperings, soft winds, mystical sunsets
and the wonderment of love

---

[1] Please feel free to substitute the word "Spirit" or "Mother" for "Father" in the above prayer.

PART II

My Path to Peace

Love is ever present
In the stillness of God

CHAPTER 7

On the Wings of Love

I spend much of my time in restaurants writing and engaging in spiritual conversations. My mom once asked me, "Couldn't you just go to the library to work?" As I thought about her question, I realized that part of the reason I go to restaurants is to interact with people.

Although I remain focused when writing, I often find myself involved in the most interesting conversations with restaurant servers. I feel so appreciative of the kindness they extend to me. Their profession is one of the highest—service to others. As they refill my glass with iced tea or ask me if I need anything, I thank them for their attentiveness. What I am most appreciative of, however, is their openness—their willingness to share.

What is especially amazing to me is that these spiritual interactions often take place in the midst of chaos, as these servers are darting back and forth between tables. It is a reminder to me that when it comes to spirituality, there are no boundaries—any time, any place. God is always present.

☙

It was a Sunday afternoon, and I was working on this book at a restaurant, a local favorite that serves traditional Cincinnati chili flavored with chocolate and cinnamon. My server, Megan, was college-aged with long brown hair and a friendly disposition. It was a wet, cool spring day, and as I talked with Megan, I learned she was ready for a nap. It was that kind of a day.

As I typed on my laptop, Megan, who had been observing me from a distance, finally asked me what I was working on. I told her it was a book about helping people to identify and appreciate their spiritual experiences. I then shared the story of a thirty-four-year-old woman named Carrie who said she had never had an identifiable spiritual experience.

Although raised Catholic, Carrie couldn't remember ever having felt unusually moved during any church service or by any other life experience. She had simply gone to church every Sunday.

Last year Carrie found herself in a deep state of depression after an emotional breakup with her boyfriend. She felt hopeless, alone, and unwanted. Although she had dealt with breakups before, this was different.

Carrie's father, who had been somewhat uninvolved and distant during her childhood, grew concerned and began calling her daily. Although he lived a couple of hours away, he started visiting her often, frequently staying for a few days at a time. Now that he was retired, his relationship with her had changed. He had more time for her and seemed more relaxed. Carrie had never seen this side of her father while growing up. In the past, his focus had been on providing financial support for his family; emotional support had always come from her mother.

Things were different now, however. When Carrie's father came to visit, he would busy himself during the day with small projects around her house. At night he would engage Carrie in conversation while they had dinner. If he sensed that Carrie was feeling sad, he would ask her if she needed a hug or ask her if she wanted to sit with him on the couch. If she chose the latter, Carrie would rest her head on his chest and watch TV ... or cry. After two months, Carrie's depression began to lift.

One day Carrie's father impulsively decided to get her a pet. She had always wanted a dog, but her father had discouraged the idea. He thought she was gone too much. Now, though, he felt the time was right and he bought her a Bichon puppy. The dog weighed two and a half pounds, and Carrie immediately fell in love with what she called her "little white fluff ball."

The puppy, which she named Coco, was a great source of comfort and companionship for Carrie. Her ever-practical father, relying on a feeling, had driven to a distant location to buy the dog for her. For this reason and others, Carrie felt destined to have received this particular animal.

Because the puppy had come from a "dirty breeder," she had multiple health issues, including a urinary-tract infection, tapeworms, and ear problems, yet Carrie didn't mind. Coco had been sent to her to be cared for.

Coco's emotional needs were easy for Carrie to satisfy; she was happy to be played with and content to be cuddled. In return, she filled a void in Carrie's life, giving her a reason to smile constantly. She reminded Carrie of the ending of her grandmother's favorite poem, titled "A Faithful Dog":

> *His blind, implicit faith in you is matched by his great love,*
> *The kind that all of us should have in the Master, up above.*
> *When everything is said and done, I guess this isn't odd,*
> *For when you spell "dog" backwards, you will get the name God.*
> —Kathryn Brashier

She had kept the poem from years earlier when her grandmother had given it to her. It was now affixed to her fridge.

When I asked Carrie if she could identify a spiritual experience she'd had, one that would cause her to step back and take pause, she came to realize that the overwhelming and surprising love that her father had shown her during this difficult time was just such an experience. It was love that seemed to have come out of nowhere at a time when she had felt the most alone and afraid. It was love that had brought her the "little white fluff ball," the most precious gift of her life. It was love that made her feel comforted and safe, to well up with emotion. And it was love that ignited a passion within her to begin reading spiritual books and to view the world differently.

As I shared this story with Megan, she told me she had a story of her own to share.

Although Megan was raised Catholic and went to church weekly, she did not consider herself to be very religious. Like Carrie, she did not get much out of going to church.

Megan lost her grandfather when she was eighteen. She used to go to her grandparents' home every Sunday for supper, and his loss brought a sense of incompleteness to what had been a comforting routine.

Megan's grandfather spent the last year of his life in a nursing home. He had Alzheimer's and Parkinson's diseases, and his wife was no longer able to care for him. On the anniversary of her grandfather's admission to the nursing home, Megan went to visit him. While there, she was told that he had an infection and wasn't doing well; the news upset her. Upon leaving under a cloud of concern for her grandfather, she noticed a beautiful orange and black monarch butterfly flitting between the flowers outside the facility.

A few days later, the nursing home called Megan's family and told them that her grandfather had taken a turn for the worse; he could pass away at any minute. Although the family received the call at 8:00 a.m., they were unable to make it to the hospital until 10:30 a.m., despite repeated urgent calls from the facility. Her grandfather died within one minute of her family's arrival, which Megan found remarkable. He had waited for them.

On the day of her grandfather's funeral, Megan saw a couple of monarch butterflies on her way into and out of the church. At the cemetery, Megan saw several more, often in clumps, but didn't think much of it. Later that day, she saw more of the butterflies at her grandparents' home and began to take notice.

The wings of the monarchs were colored in multiple shades of orange with black outlining the edges and streaking up the center. The wingtips had splotches of yellow and tones of deep red while white dots lined the outer edges in contrast to the black. As the butterflies rested and tried to steady themselves against the wind, their delicate, paper-thin wings moved backwards to balance them, almost folding against the pressure; yet when they flew, their wings fluttered rhythmically and powerfully as they glided from flower to flower.

Since her grandfather's funeral, Megan has come to appreciate some unusual associations with monarch butterflies. She plays soccer for a local university, and whenever she notices one of the orange and black beauties, her team always seems to win. It has now gotten to the point where the girls on the team get excited as soon as they see a monarch, shouting to Megan, "Oh my God! We're going to win!"

Every time Megan is struggling through a bad day, monarchs seem to magically appear. Sometimes small white and yellow butterflies surround them. As she is sitting in class, thinking she doesn't want to be there, or driving home on a cold and gloomy day, Megan will look outside, see one of those strikingly colorful butterflies, and suddenly find herself smiling.

Megan knew she would be facing a difficult time when she had to undergo surgery for an injured knee. On the day of her pre-op exam, she was feeling distraught. It was summertime, right before the beginning of soccer season, and Megan had earned a starting position. Unfortunately, because of her injury, she was going to be sidelined. Megan was crying as she left the medical center, but her perspective changed when she encountered a monarch. She immediately felt soothed and relaxed, surprisingly calm and reassured. She knew it was going to be all right; this was just something she had to go through.

As Megan shared this story with me, she repeatedly stated, "I don't believe in this sort of thing."

She later told me that she said this so I wouldn't think she was crazy. It was hard for her to ignore the evidence.

Coincidentally, as I sat at the restaurant interacting with Megan, I had a copy of the book *Inspiration—Your Ultimate Calling* by Wayne Dyer. In this uplifting book, Wayne speaks at length about a deceased friend of his who was enamored with monarch butterflies. His friend would tell people how multiple generations of these delicate butterflies travel thousands of miles on round trips from Brazil to Nova Scotia, only to come back to the same tree and the same branch from which their ancestors had emerged. Wayne describes how one of these butterflies once came and stayed with him for a couple of hours, happily perched on his finger. He believed it was his old friend visiting him.

As I handed the book to Megan as a gift, it was hard for her to miss the picture of the monarch butterfly on its cover. She seemed somewhat mesmerized as she turned it over, only to discover three more monarchs on the back cover. A look of wonderment appeared on her face as her eyes moistened with tears. Her grandfather's butterflies were everywhere, and they had come to visit her.

The spirit of love
The essence of God
Is found through our appreciation
Of life's beating heart

A heart that pulsates
In every life form
With the beauty, the purity
Of the Holy Spirit

CHAPTER 8

The Power of Spirit

Not long after hearing Megan's story, I had my own encounter with butterflies during a challenging time. On a Friday afternoon, my wife, Raye Ann, went to see her gastroenterologist after experiencing some lower-abdominal discomfort. During the exam, he discovered a mass, and she was scheduled for a colonoscopy the following Monday. I had planned to take my children, David and Suzanne, to Ocean City, New Jersey, the next day, but I stayed with Raye Ann and sent the kids off with my brother, Michael.

Early Saturday morning, Raye Ann and I decided to go for a hike. When we left the house, I noticed that every tree was swaying with life and spirit. I couldn't help but feel that God was communicating with us. As we walked along a trail at a local park, my attention was drawn to numerous small black and orange butterflies that looked like miniature monarchs. They seemed to be leading us everywhere. They would land on the path in front of us and, as we approached, would soar ahead only to rest once again on the path directly ahead. I began to understand that we were not alone. In these challenging moments, God was making his presence known. I felt joy, peace, and hope. It was not that we were being assured of a specific outcome for Raye Ann but rather that God was there to comfort and guide us, to remind us that on a spiritual level there was nothing to fear.

As we continued along the path, I excitedly shared my observations with Raye Ann—spirit was speaking the language of love. Shortly thereafter, a butterfly landed on me. After a couple of seconds, it flew away, only to land on me again five feet further down the trail. This unusual occurrence happened several more times.

During this time, I also saw a monarch butterfly. Although I had previously seen yellow and black butterflies that strikingly resembled the monarch in these woods, this was the first true monarch I had noticed. I couldn't help but remember Megan's story, her feeling after her pre-op physical that everything would be okay, that this was just something she had to go through. I smiled to myself and felt a similar reassurance that Raye Ann would be okay, that this was just a path she needed to travel. The signs were overwhelming. God was everywhere.

On Monday we received good news. Raye Ann's mass, at least on colonoscopy, appeared to be benign, although biopsies were still pending. Later that afternoon, a caring friend extended her sympathies to me for the difficult days my wife and I must have endured prior to the procedure. I replied that I very much appreciated her concern, but our experience had been quite the opposite; Raye Ann and I had enjoyed a beautiful weekend listening to the voice of God, the music of love, and the whisperings of the monarch.

The following day as I was writing about our butterflies, I received a call from Raye Ann's gastroenterologist. He told me that her biopsy from the previous afternoon had revealed cancer. I was caught off guard. I had not expected the results to be available so quickly and hurried home to comfort Raye Ann.

On my arrival, I could tell she had been crying. She felt

overwhelmed. We had been married for seventeen years, and looking at her reminded me of the deep love and respect I felt for her. From very early on in our relationship, I knew she was the one person for me, my soul mate. Although she had a strong personality, reminiscent of a mother polar bear, she also possessed a vulnerable, childlike innocence that I found endearing. It was my job to take care of her, and it was a job that I relished—not from a standpoint of dependency but from one of empowerment, guiding her back to her beautiful light within, especially when the overwhelming noise of fear distracted her.

I reminded her of my initial feeling that this was just something she would have to go through, but that in the end, everything would be fine. Surprisingly enough, within ten minutes her perspective changed. She seemed to be reconnecting with the spiritual peace she had experienced before her biopsy. On some level, she knew her path was being guided.

Later that day as her doctor's nurse advised her to schedule a chest and abdominal CT scan, she once again broke down. Reality had a way of making it hard to stay on that spiritual plane. The talk of the CT scan had increased her fear that the cancer had spread. I told her it didn't matter; I knew she would be okay. I could already see the end of the movie, and it was good. Everything else was just drama.

That night as I headed up to the hospital to pick up the contrast for her CT scan, I asked God to verify that my feelings were correct. I did not want to give Raye Ann false information or false hope.

On my return, Raye Ann told me she had called her sister, Mary Gail, to tell her about the cancer diagnosis. At first her sister did not respond; there was only a prolonged silence. Mary Gail later related that, during that silence, she had felt a sensation of complete peace descend upon her, leaving her with a "knowing" that everything would be all right.

When I heard about Mary Gail's experience, I knew that God had given me the confirmation I was seeking. I felt elated and appreciative.

I understood that Raye Ann not only would endure this experience but that it would be a positive life-changing event as well.

I was amazed at how peaceful Raye Ann was during the first few days following her diagnosis. Aside from occasionally feeling overwhelmed, the majority of her time was spent in a tranquil state. This was surprising since she had long struggled with depression and often felt her life lacked purpose, but despite this recent diagnosis of cancer, Raye Ann spent a considerable amount of time editing my book, something that required concentration and clarity of mind.

During this period, we enjoyed many of the same pleasurable activities we had before the biopsy. We watched humorous movies, ate nice meals, and went for enjoyable walks. I felt closer to Raye Ann than ever before.

Raye Ann told me she felt there were now two parts to her life, the part before cancer and the part afterwards. I agreed with her. I felt that everything in her life prior to her diagnosis had led up to this moment, that she was preparing to begin the second phase.

I explained to her that I thought this second phase was something to be embraced. I understood intuitively that Raye Ann was getting ready to soar spiritually, to move to a higher level. I knew that she would be challenged at times, but I also knew that I would be there for her and that in the end she would have a clearer sense of her purpose and her light. She would walk the path of love, and God would tenderly hold her hand while accompanying her on this faith-filled journey.

Raye Ann received two courses of chemotherapy and six weeks of radiation. During her six-week treatment, she soared with spirit in ways she never dreamed possible. She was often smiling, funny, radiant, and optimistic. She chose to minimize her focus on any discomfort she was experiencing and relied on her faith to lead her in higher directions. Despite a severe case of mouth ulcerations, she remained tranquil and centered, treating the ulcerations as a mere distraction as she ate strawberry Jell-O and read inspirational books. In her hospital room, she imagined herself being comforted by a prayer quilt—a quilt knitted with all of the healing prayers that had been extended on her behalf, one constructed of much love and consideration. Upon her discharge from the hospital, Raye Ann elected to ride home in an open convertible, embracing life with heightened energy and ever appreciative of the light breeze and sunny sky.

Raye Ann's most challenging situations were unanticipated events that occurred after her treatment—for example, an unexpected and tearful hospitalization for a fever and low white blood count that was preceded by shaking chills at a hair salon as she excitedly prepared for out-of-town family. Although less discomforting and serious than her treatment experiences, these events were more challenging emotionally and spiritually because they were unanticipated. They reminded Raye Ann of the power of spirit, of the differences in one's experiences when approaching healing with purpose and faith as opposed to focusing on the fear of uncertainty and the disappointment of unmet expectations.

Raye Ann's six-month follow-up study showed no sign of residual cancer. After the procedure, she spoke of an experience she had had earlier that morning. She had received a spiritual communication confirming that her cancer was gone and would not recur. I asked her if she would have paid attention to such a feeling several years ago, before we began the spiritual endeavor of writing this book. She told me that several years ago she wouldn't have even noticed it.

"What made the difference?" I asked. "What enabled you to soar for those six weeks?"

After much consideration, Raye Ann responded, "I completely surrendered and gave total control of the treatment and outcome to God."

She then added, "In retrospect, the week I was diagnosed with cancer was one of the best weeks of my life. I never felt closer to God or to you. I never felt more energized!"

As we search for beauty
In the midst of hardship
We begin to understand and appreciate

C H A P T E R 9

The Story of My Journey

I was baptized in the Greek Orthodox Church. Although my family regularly went to church as I was growing up, my religious experience was limited because the Mass was largely conducted in Greek, a language I did not understand. Our church was a half hour from home, and Mass lasted close to two hours. My favorite early church experiences often involved food, since on Sunday mornings my parents would regularly entice us to go to service with the promise of a nice lunch. Lunch meant eating at a nearby cafeteria that served hand-carved roast beef or at an up-and-coming fast-food restaurant that prepared its hamburgers with the unique taste of pickles, chopped onions, mustard, and ketchup. To this day, much of my spiritual writing and many of my spiritual conversations still take place in restaurants, where I can slowly sip iced tea and quiet the noise of the outside world.

The Greek Orthodox services were steeped in tradition. I remember enjoying the musky scent of incense as the priest swung an ornate burner throughout Mass. The vessel was always swung three times, symbolizing the Holy Trinity of the Father, Son, and Holy Spirit. To me, this symbolism spoke of the multidimensional and mysterious nature of God, a simple but intriguing concept that was rich with theological complexities and interwoven with love, peace, and joy.

One of my favorite services was the midnight Mass preceding Easter Sunday when the darkened church slowly became alive with light as one candle lit another against a backdrop of beautiful music and the eventual singing of "Christos Anesti" ("Christ Has Risen"). This left me with a feeling of excitement and wonderment, a feeling that lingered during wonderful 2:00 a.m. breakfasts at a local restaurant.

By junior high, I had begun to feel a stronger connection with the church and with God. I especially liked outdoor guitar masses at summer camp. The services were casual. The surrounding forest, teeming with songbirds, made for a peaceful, spiritual environment that left me feeling warm and comforted. By the time I reached sixteen, my church experiences had imbued in me a deep feeling of peace and love.

I remember being particularly fond of a small crucifix that hung on a gold chain that I had received as a gift. The chain's thin, delicate nature appeared fragile, but its links were surprisingly sturdy. It reflected my perception of Jesus, meek appearing but strength filled.

The crucifix itself was a one-and-a-half-inch dark wooden cross adorned with a finely detailed gold replica of Jesus. Its makeup and the fact that I wore it close to my heart signified something powerful to me—it presented a physical image of my intimate relationship with this tender-hearted man of faith. I treasured that cross and knew that my feelings toward the cross were symbolic of my love of the church and of Christ.

As a freshman in college, I frequently attended Catholic masses on Sunday evenings. The guitar masses were held in a contemporary white chapel with gleaming oak floors and an abundance of glass. I attended the services with a friend, who like me was still trying to find her way in life. Although I felt pressured to spend my Sunday nights studying and preparing papers, I felt more content going to church than catching up on schoolwork. Religion continued to bring a feeling of serenity to my life.

During the second semester of my freshman year, a number of

events took place that caused me to question my beliefs and the teachings of organized religion. I took a course titled Contemporary American Problems in which we studied poverty, global hunger, and other topics that I found disturbing. As we examined racial discrimination, abusive government practices, and other problems that illustrated man's inhumanity to man, I found myself becoming very upset by the human inequities prevalent in our modern society. I was uncertain if I wanted to live in a world so full of hurt and injustice. It was during this period in my life that I came to understand the effects of mental depression—the feeling of having so little energy that you literally couldn't move. I remember feeling so sad, so deflated, that at times I couldn't muster the energy even to do a load of laundry.

During this same period, I read James Joyce's semi-autobiographical novel, *A Portrait of the Artist as a Young Man,* for an English literature class. In one part of the book, a preacher describes the depths of hell to his congregation. He graphically details the intense pain and suffering of unrepentant sinners enduring the anguish of an uncompromising and eternal fiery hell. Although I didn't particularly believe that hell existed, I remember being troubled by the lengthy passage. It evoked feelings of fear and guilt and reminded me of the non-spiritual side of religion. I found it hard to understand why religion chose to motivate people through fear rather than through the light of love.

Around the same time, I remember returning home for a weekend and having a discussion about evolution with my father. My father, a caring physician who loved science, wondered whether religion was more of a social creation than a spiritual reality. Although religion performed many useful psychological and social functions, in his eyes the scientific evidence appeared to be contradictory. Without drawing definite conclusions, he left me pondering whether we evolved from more primitive animal species and, if we did, whether this was compatible with religious creationist ideas. Toward the end of his life, my father, while always connected with love, became more intrigued with religion and more awakened to God—due, in part, to his viewing of the film *The Passion of Christ*.

By the end of my freshman year, I had begun to have serious religious doubts and conflicting beliefs. They did not arise from a lack of spiritual love, as I had often felt peaceful and connected in church, but rather from a difficulty reconciling religious teachings with all of the suffering in the world. How could an all-powerful and loving God allow such immense suffering, especially that of young innocent children and frail elderly adults? I wondered whether our belief in God was more a result of wishful thinking than of higher reasoning. I also had many questions about the fear and guilt associated with religion and how to reconcile the theory of evolution with creationism.

After my freshman year, I became an agnostic. I decided to focus my attention on being true to myself and to my values. After all, if God is love, shouldn't expressing love be the priority? Why would I necessarily have to believe in God if I were connected with love and truth?

I had always been intrigued by Eastern religious thought and practice, and in my junior year I took advantage of an opportunity to learn how to meditate. During meditation, I became more relaxed as my stress dissipated. At times I would go into a dreamlike, euphoric state in which I felt total peace—at other times I would feel an underlying restlessness and focus on my breathing as time passed ever so slowly.

Over the years, I continued to remain unsure of the existence of God even though I strongly identified with Christ's values and love for humanity and felt an inexplicable peace about death. I did have experiences that were spiritual in nature, but I failed to recognize them as such.

I remember attending a service for my nephew's first communion in 1999. As I sat in the church, I was enveloped by a peaceful serenity filled with so much love that time appeared to stand still. It was reminiscent of the feelings I'd had during guitar masses at summer camp and at college. It gave me pause.

During the spring of 2001, I began interacting with a patient who changed the course of my life. John had been receiving communications about future events that were causing him distress. On one occasion, he entered a friend's home and felt as if he were walking into a funeral parlor. Shortly thereafter, someone in the house passed. On another occasion, he sensed that his sister would be dying soon. Five days later, after seeing a doctor and receiving a clean bill of health, she died from a stroke.

As John described these events, I was moved by his story. He was seeing me not to validate his perceptions but because of the fear and unease these communications were causing him. It was as if he had tapped into another dimension, one that left him feeling decidedly uncomfortable and vulnerable. As he recounted his experiences, I suddenly felt the universe come alive with light.

I was jolted awake!

I realized that if the future could be foretold, there was more to life than I had previously imagined. I began sensing the presence of a spiritual energy in the universe. It was a strangely familiar feeling—of coming home to something mysterious, captivating, and alluring. I was being reacquainted with an ancient and rich language—one that I had once spoken fluently but had long since forgotten.

I started reading spiritual books. Early on I was especially influenced by Raymond A. Moody Jr.'s *Life After Life*. In this book, Dr. Moody objectively describes the near-death experiences of a number of people who spoke of interacting with a warm, beautiful, and radiant light, a light of perfect understanding and love, a *being* of light, an entity, that would forever change their understanding of the world around them.

As I continued to read a number of books on near-death experiences, I encountered further testimonials to support a universe that is directed by a higher intelligence of love, peace, and spiritual growth.

Closer to the Light, by Melvin Morse, MD, wonderfully describes the near-death experiences of children. I also read books from mediums like John Edwards. I found his first book, *One Last Time,* to be both believable and intriguing. I enjoyed reading about his spiritual experiences in childhood when he first became aware of his psychic abilities. These experiences included seeing colorful auras around his elementary school teachers, knowing how to get to places to which he had never been, being intimately familiar with family matters that predated his birth, and feeling sad and irritable for several days before major world tragedies.

Over the next year and a half, I had an insatiable appetite for any spiritual material. Some authors, such as Neale Donald Walsch, Wayne Dyer, Eckhart Tolle, and James Redfield, were less traditional than others but were always inspiring and empowering. Their writings spoke to my heart.

Neale Walsch's writings emphasized our wonderful creative powers—that is, how much our thoughts, words, and actions affect the world around us. Eckhart Tolle's writings focused on quieting our minds—minds that are racing out of control with thoughts of the past and future and that keep us from feeling the love and peace of the moment. Wayne Dyer spoke of our intimate connection with the universe—a universe that is responsive to our intentions and our energy. And James Redfield discussed the importance of awareness—of our ability to receive spiritual guidance from within and outside of ourselves; of our need to be aware of the synchronicity, the perfectly timed coincidences, occurring in our lives; and of the opportunity for each of us to interact with our magnificent *energy*-rich world.

I also read hundreds of books from other authors, all of which helped me to grow spiritually. Just as I felt I had a clear understanding of a topic, I would read something else that would add another dimension to and encourage a deeper appreciation of the subject.

During this period, I also began to have an increasing number of spiritual discussions and to feel more spiritually empowered. No matter what the topic of conversation, I would usually bring up some spiritual question or issue. It was as if I had an unquenchable thirst for any information on the topic. Like a dormant tree at the end of winter, I was undergoing a rebirth. It was time for me to grow and blossom.

I started asking patients in my medical practice about their spiritual experiences after the deaths of loved ones. Their responses amazed me. Many of them had experienced events that clearly pointed to some type of communication from the deceased. Recalling one such experience, a couple told me that they had seen a poster fly off the wall in a bar, smack a friend of theirs in the face, and then reattach itself to the wall, reminding them of an event involving their recently deceased friend. In a number of other circumstances, lights flickered, multiple lightbulbs burned out, or a bright light from an unknown source radiated warmth on anniversaries or other meaningful occasions. These patients often said they had not shared these experiences with anyone else for fear of looking ridiculous. I felt privileged that they were willing to share their stories with me. In some way I felt I was able to help them to validate their feelings and beliefs.

I remember talking on the phone to a friend who mentioned that an electrician was working in her basement. The electrician had recently lost his three-year-old son. I asked my friend to ask him if he had felt any communication from his son since his death. He told her they had buried his son with the play phone that he had always carried around. Since that time the electrician kept feeling his beeper vibrate, but there was no call back number. He continued to feel the vibration even when the beeper was turned off. He was sure it was his son communicating with him.

It seemed that wherever I looked there was evidence for post-death communication. These communications often served to bring great comfort and spiritual peace to those still on earth by reminding them of the eternal connection to their loved ones and to the spiritual universe.

One day as I was driving to work listening to "O Little Town of

Bethlehem," a feeling of intense love and joy came over me. It was a remarkable sensation—one I had never experienced. It was a feeling of absolute peace and breathtaking beauty. I was reminded of lazy sunsets and flowers glistening with morning dew, of soft-flowing tears that speak of love and forgiveness, of an outstretched hand, warm and inviting. It was a feeling of immeasurable sweetness. It was God.

Embedded in this heightened feeling of love was a message—"Give!"—give without limits—give freely and openly—give from the depth of your soul!

I will never forget the experience of that morning, of the gentleness of God's love, nor will I ever forget the messages that accompanied the feeling, to give generously and from the heart.

I am forever grateful for the experiences that spiritual love has brought me as I continue along this road. I have come to trust and rely on my intuition as never before. If I feel I should do something that is in some way spiritually inspired, I usually will do so ... at least eventually.

On a flight from Orlando, for example, I had the feeling I should talk to the man sitting next to me. Although probably in his early fifties, Cliff looked like he was in his late thirties. I couldn't help but notice his boyish charm as he flirted and joked around with some of the younger women on the flight. He reminded me of the all-American boy, fully grown but forever youthful—multitalented in sports, music, and any other field he tackled.

I could tell Cliff was someone who embraced life and never took things too seriously; however, I could also tell he was someone who understood the spiritual nature of the universe and the joy of service. While we chatted, Cliff described an unusual experience he'd had as a military pilot during the Vietnam War. As he was beginning his aerial dive to attack a convoy of tanks, he realized there were soldiers fighting closely alongside the tanks. When his jet descended further, he noticed the men fighting near the tanks were actually chained to them. Seeing this caused Cliff great consternation. The fate of these men was tied directly to the tanks to which they were enslaved. They had no choice but to fight, yet this wasn't the way things were supposed to be. The episode caused Cliff to question the way he viewed life and the spiritual universe.

I haven't spoken with Cliff since our flight together. I never asked him if he attacked those tanks, and if so, how it made him feel. I was too focused on watching his face, his thoughtful expression, as he described the experience—imagining him reexamining his life and his principles in the solitude of his military jet, thousands of feet in the air, moving at supersonic speeds—sensing that the experience led him to a state of increased awareness and compassion.

৶

As I continue on my spiritual path, I find there is so much to learn, so much to appreciate. My prayers now begin with an intention to allow love to enter my heart ... to see and feel the beauty that surrounds and encompasses me. By blessing myself—praying for myself—my cup fills with love and begins to overflow. As love spills forth, my ability to commune with others increases. I become a more effective instrument of God.

A Prayer for Spiritual Receptivity

That I may be humble in my demeanor
Patient in my interactions
Courageous in my endeavors
And gentle in my questioning

Appreciative in manner
Embracing of light
Receptive to guidance
And open to love

PART III

Quieting the Noise

God's plan is not our plan
God's time is not our time
But God never arrives late

—Father Steve Angi

CHAPTER 10

Spiritual Love Beckons.
We Need Only Listen.

*E*ven though we may be unaware of it, spiritual love communicates with us on a constant basis. The secret to hearing God is to quiet our minds. By turning down the outside noise, we become more receptive to spiritual communication. This communication can come to us through a vast array of different media, including music, art, books, poetry, prayer, meditation, nature, and places of worship. It can also come through a common but unexpected medium—other people. Have you ever listened to someone talking to you and felt as if God were speaking to you through him or her? Or have you ever been the person speaking and felt as if it were your voice coming out but not your thoughts?

One day in particular, I felt as if a number of patients were communicating spiritual truths to me as they talked about their life experiences. It was intriguing because their stories were so freely and enthusiastically given. Listening to them mesmerized me. They spoke with love, compassion, and faith in the human spirit.

One such patient, Heinz, started talking about his days as a soccer coach. Heinz was responsible for helping to bring youth soccer to Cincinnati. As I listened to him, I realized he was also talking about life.

Heinz spoke with great love about his commitment to the kids and the sport. It was easy to see that he wanted every child on his team to become empowered through soccer.

This man with a large family had balanced work, family, and coaching because of his giving nature. He told me he expected a lot from the kids and that he was strict. I came to realize that by "strict" he meant only that he wanted the players to reach their potential. Heinz expected his kids to be punctual, but if anyone needed transportation, he freely provided it. He spent plenty of time with the weaker players who began to display pride in themselves as they developed their skills. They quickly learned that if they tried their best, it didn't matter if they made mistakes. It wasn't about perfection; it was about effort. Heinz also focused on teamwork, in particular, team communication. After every match, he would ask all the players to share their feelings about the game.

Heinz treated the kids as if they were his own because that is how he felt about them. It made no difference whether they were American-born or foreign, rich or poor. Each child was treated as an individual.

As I listened to Heinz, I felt as if I were listening to someone reading a book about spiritual coaching. He coached with love, and he truly cared about every individual child on his team. He taught his kids many skills along the way, but most of all he taught them about empowerment. In the process, he enabled a number of "champions" to celebrate themselves.

ༀ

Spiritual love communicates in many ways. The most direct way is through *feelings*. That is why I believe so strongly that we should pay close attention to our intuition. When I first began this project,

I didn't think I had the knowledge or the talent to write a book. This undertaking resulted from a feeling I had to express my spiritual truths. Along the way I hoped to learn more about myself and, ideally, to generate discussions that would enlighten me as to the spiritual beliefs of others. So far, the experience has been both wonderful and challenging. I have received a great deal of support and love from an array of different people.

At times when I haven't been sure of how to proceed, I have had to step back and wait for further direction and insight. By going inward and quieting my mind, I have been able to reconnect.

❦

Linda related an experience that had happened to her a number of years ago. She had just gone through a divorce after discovering her husband was having an affair. She had subsequently moved to another city with her three young children and had begun the process of returning to school and starting a new job. Although Linda had tried to lead a good spiritual life, she felt her life was unraveling.

At one point, Linda became overwhelmed. She felt forsaken by God and began screaming obscenities at him. As she railed at God, however, a little voice told her it was exactly at these times of hopelessness that she needed to *lean* on him. Linda considered ignoring the voice but instead reached for her Bible and opened it.

When she looked down at the worn pages, her eyes immediately fell on a passage in Job (38:2):

> *Who is this that speaks with words without knowledge?*
> *Answer me, for I will question you like a man.*
> *Where were you when I laid the earth's foundation?*

The passage took her breath away. Linda felt her hair stand on end as if a lightning bolt had struck her! She sensed the gentle chiding of a velvet hand touch her face.

In that instant, Linda understood that the accusatory words she had hurled at God, the curses she had uttered, were spoken "without knowledge." They were not the language of spirit—a language of beauty and creation—but hurtful words arising from fear and rage.

Upon this immediate realization—this sudden awakening—Linda began to experience the inviting warmth of God's presence. Her eyes flooded with tears as she became immersed in the joy of God's love.

Linda still regrets not trusting her earlier feeling to lean on God. When she reflects on that passage and the special meaning it continues to hold for her, she once again is brought to tears, humbled anew. Like a child kneeling to pray, her soul naked and vulnerable, she revels in the simple truth—*love is, and always will be, the way.*

ॐ

I have found that we receive considerable guidance as we go about our lives. We just need to learn to be quiet enough to listen. We might feel an impulse to be more generous with a street person, to express words of love or thanks to someone, to call a friend, or to offer assistance to someone less fortunate. I believe it is important for us to act on these impulses before our more reality-based, less-spiritual mind tells us not to. I doubt that, as we reflect on our lives, we will ever wish we had been less giving or less loving. Acting on these impulses is a reflection of our true loving nature.

ॐ

On a fall evening, while waiting for my daughter to finish basketball practice, I went to a Mediterranean restaurant that specializes in gourmet pizza. As the college-aged hostess seated me, I asked her how her day was going. It was a cold and drizzly Sunday night, and she told me she'd had a horrible weekend.

After ordering, I had the feeling I should do something to try to improve her mood. I decided to visit the bookstore next door.

Upon entering the shop, I was drawn to a petite box of gourmet chocolates and a picture frame with a quote from Helen Keller etched into its metallic border. The quote read:

The most beautiful experiences in the world
cannot be seen or even touched
they must be felt within the heart

I put both articles in a small colorful gift bag.

When I reentered the restaurant, I spotted the hostess kneeling on a seat cushion, wiping down a table. I went over to her, handed her the bag, and said, "This is for you since you had such a difficult weekend." She hardly looked up at me, thanking me in a way that expressed little interest.

As I walked away, I wondered how this would play out. The hostess could easily take my actions the wrong way. She was an attractive young woman, and I was there by myself, but I had come to a point in my life where I trusted my intuition. I decided to simply focus on my writing and enjoy my dinner. Although I saw the hostess several more times during the evening, we never made eye contact.

At the end of my dinner as I was getting ready to leave, she came over to my table. She was smiling, and her eyes were moist. She told me she really appreciated the gifts; they totally changed the way she had been feeling.

She went on to tell me that her boyfriend had broken up with her on the Friday before and things had worsened over the weekend, but that her perspective had changed after she'd had a chance to look at the gifts.

As I looked into her tear-filled eyes, I felt as if I were peering into the soul of God—so much love and appreciation for such a simple gift. I stood up and gave her a hug.

I asked her if she had read the inscription on the frame. She said she had, and we went on to talk about the quote. I voiced my thoughts about how the beauty of life is all around us and how this beauty is best appreciated when our minds are quiet. She listened and smiled. I asked her if she liked to read, and she told me she did.

I decided to go back to the bookstore and get her the book *The Alchemist*, by Paulo Coelho. *The Alchemist* is a fable that explains how the whole universe conspires to help us when we follow our dreams or personal legends. It talks of omens, wonderful signs that are meant to help us along our path. It also mentions the universal language, "the language of enthusiasm, of things accomplished with love and purpose, and as part of a search for something believed in and desired." It was my hope that the book would further empower her and enable her to connect spiritually. As I handed her the book, she thanked me.

Leaving the restaurant, I couldn't help but remember the look in her eyes when she had first expressed her appreciation to me. Her eyes radiated the gentle spirit of God—a spirit of innocence, humility, and, most strikingly, love.

As we learn to quiet our minds and trust our feelings
Our intuition becomes our guiding light
We are comforted by the realization
That we are one with the spirit of life

CHAPTER 11

Trust Your Intuition

I define "intuition" as a feeling one gets about something or someone without an identifiable reason as to why the feeling exists. It
is said that we rely more on our other senses, but our sixth sense, our
intuition, is actually much more powerful.

I asked Father Steve how he thought we could maximize our
intuition—whether there were certain techniques that, if used over
a period of time, might strengthen our ability to be intuitive. He
said we best utilize our intuition by being in touch with ourselves
and with others. He went on to say that as we come to understand
our purpose in life, we naturally become more in touch with our
intuition.

I would suggest that the more we can quiet the mind and listen
to ourselves and others, the more effectively we can utilize one of
our grandest and most intriguing gifts. As each of us makes use of
techniques—prayer, music, reading, exercise, nature, and so on—to
strengthen our connectedness, our minds become still and more responsive to our sixth sense. When we fully utilize our intuition, we
are able to pick up signals from sources we might otherwise ignore.
More importantly, I believe our intuition is in touch with the spiritual

energy of the universe and can guide us along our path in the most extraordinary manner.

☙

While out shopping during the Christmas season, Kathy stopped at a pet store to purchase some items for her cat. On her way out of the store, she took a moment to look at some rescue animals located near the exit, but as she started to walk away, a voice in her right ear told her to return—to "go back in" and proceed down a certain aisle. She didn't understand. She had bought what she had come for, and besides, she'd already spent all of her holiday money, but she reentered the store and walked down the aisle to which she was directed, where she saw even more rescue animals.

She felt drawn to one puppy in particular, a small terrier with soft, dark brown eyes. The puppy was solid black with white stripes down her belly and a few white hairs on her chin. As Kathy picked her up, the terrier affectionately licked her face. Although she was quite taken with the puppy, she wasn't looking for a dog. She had always been a cat person. After putting the terrier down and walking away, Kathy noticed she was continuing to bark and jump up and down against the fence. Kathy felt that same inner voice calling her back. She returned to the puppy … then tried, once again, to walk away. This happened repeatedly for some time—Kathy gradually drawing away and then being pulled back to play with the terrier. After a while she wondered, *What is going on? What am I doing?*

An hour later, Kathy realized she couldn't leave without the puppy. She had no money with her, so she told the salespeople that if they wanted her to take the dog, she would have to go home or to a bank to get the seventy-five-dollar adoption fee. In any event, she wasn't leaving the store without the animal. At first the store employees weren't sure what to do, but finally they told her to take the terrier for free. They trusted that the dog was going to a good home. Within a few minutes, Kathy signed the ownership papers and left the store with her new pet.

After arriving home, Kathy wondered what had come over her. She knew absolutely nothing about taking care of a puppy. Her first couple of weeks were challenging. The terrier, which she named Tsana, was a "holy terror!" Yet it was hard for Kathy to stay upset with the dog; its mannerisms were too cute. If Kathy yelled at Tsana, she would playfully roll over and expose her soft belly, as if asking for forgiveness while coyly inviting Kathy to rub and scratch her.

Kathy, who was naturally shy, had lived in the same house for quite a while. It wasn't until Tsana's arrival, however, that she had much interaction with her neighbors. When she walked the puppy down the street, people would slow down and wave. Children would come up to her and ask her if they could pet Tsana, afterward saying, "I really love your dog!" On one occasion, a van pulled by with an elderly gentleman sitting on the passenger side. As he looked out and saw Tsana, a big smile spread across his face.

Kathy's mother became excited when she heard about the puppy. Whenever she talked to Kathy, she would always ask, "How's that little doggie?" If Kathy visited her mother and didn't bring the terrier with her, her mother would be disappointed. Like a favorite grandchild, she couldn't get enough of Tsana.

The atmosphere at home changed as well. Tsana's take-charge and confident attitude brought an increased energy and life to the house. Kathy's cat, Athan, became more outgoing, no longer staying in one room. He also became more affectionate, licking Kathy whenever the opportunity arose. He enjoyed showing off in front of Tsana. After bounding down the steps, he would "bounce" across the living room and eventually slide into the gate next to Tsana. Over time, Kathy became aware of a different feeling around her household. While Kathy and Athan watched Tsana playfully entertain herself in the backyard, she discovered a newfound sense of intimacy and comfort—the warm embrace of family.

Kathy's life had changed in many ways since she'd brought little Tsana home. As she moved into uncharted territories, opportunities were blossoming. She had to smile—God was both fascinating and mysterious. She had listened to the whisperings of spirit, of Christmas tidings, and now was dancing with the *light of love*.

☙

On four occasions, Vickie has been overcome with a strong feeling to be with a very sick relative or friend.

In every instance, Vickie immediately stopped what she was doing. Upon driving to see each person, Vickie's car filled with the scent of fresh flowers—as if dozens of roses were resting on the backseat.

During three of the occurrences, the person had been in a comatose state for at least two weeks, but when Vickie arrived, the loved one awakened and looked at her with "wide-open eyes." Vicki took that time to let the loved one know it was time to go and to assure the person that she would take care of any unfinished business.

Vickie fondly remembers each loved one dying in her company—just the two of them sharing an intimate moment together. After each person passed, Vickie always felt as if she were being watched. She felt the presence of many loving souls around her.

Vickie has always been hesitant to share these experiences with anyone because they were so meaningful and personal. She has never felt significant grief over the death of a loved one since she knows their souls continue to exist in a most peaceful and loving place.

Reflecting upon our life and wondering why
We have spent so much of it afraid

Living in fear of yesterday's regrets
And tomorrow's uncertainties
Life passes us by

To break fear's hold
We need only focus
On the love we have within

Then we are free
To reclaim our life
Then we are free
To truly live

—Raye Ann Sifri

CHAPTER 12

Ask Yourself: Is This Thought Love-Based or Fear-Based?

Many of our thoughts arise from either love or fear. Our life experience changes as we begin to pay attention to the types of thoughts we are having at any given time. Fear-based thoughts are those that lead to feelings of anxiety, worry, distrust, guilt, anger, depression, and hate. Love-based thoughts, on the other hand, lead to feelings of joy, peace, hope, compassion, trust, and empathy.

The noise overpowers us, and we become fearful. Yet when we quiet our minds and listen, we are reminded of the voice of God—the voice of love.

༃

A number of years ago, I began having lunches with Steve Angi, a Catholic priest and former patient of mine. Steve's experiences have included counseling teenage girls at a Catholic high school, spending time in impoverished areas of Africa, Australia, and South America, teaching English and psychology at a Chinese university, becoming well versed in paranormal experiences in New Orleans, working with street gangs throughout the United States, and serving as a probation officer in order to help control the drug traffic in one of his parish's neighborhood. He currently serves as vicar general and chancellor of the Archdiocese of Cincinnati after having earned a degree in canon law from the Catholic University of America in Washington, DC.

Steve is in his midfifties, slender, and of medium height. His tanned skin, piercing yet warm green eyes, short grayish-black hair, and quick smile all contribute to his youthful appearance. His lean figure is the result of a health-conscious lifestyle, which includes getting up around five in the morning, meditating for forty-five minutes, and then running three to four miles or working out. When we meet, he is usually wearing a light-colored polo-type shirt and casual pants, attire that reflects his easygoing and untraditional manner.

My lunches with Steve and our assorted guests have always been unpredictable. I initially thought the lunches would provide opportunities for Steve and me to hear about the spiritual beliefs of many different individuals. What I found, instead, was that many of these people had more questions than answers. This made for quite lively and varied discussions.

One day at a lunch gathering, Steve and I met an acquaintance of mine who was struggling with her marriage. Ashley had been married for several years but was yearning for a more intimate relationship with her husband, one in which she could share her deepest thoughts and feelings. Ashley met her husband, David, when she was in college. At the time, she was drawn to his generosity, his willingness to help her financially. No one had cared for Ashley this way before. She had grown up in a family in which she had to provide for many of her own material needs. She remembers sitting outside her grandmother's locked house with her younger brother and sister. They were hungry and begging their grandmother for food. Eventually they were given one bologna sandwich—to share. Later, as she lay on her bed trying to fall asleep, the hunger pains returned, a not uncommon occurrence. She recalls working the nightshift on a factory conveyor belt during the last four months of high school. She would leave the factory at 7:00 a.m. to go to school, sacrificing sleep for a college opportunity.

Things were different now. Ashley had financial security and a house full of beautiful things, but she wasn't happy. When she felt sad, she would run up her credit cards buying clothing from specialty shops or shoes from upscale department stores. Although the shopping distracted her, it didn't fill the void. It simply created marital stress and accentuated her emptiness within.

With time, Ashley came to feel like a trophy wife. She was one more item on her husband's checklist: a beautiful house, a nice car, an attractive spouse. While Ashley struggled to find meaning in her life, David was on a different path. He would rise early on Saturday mornings to work on the house, scrubbing the baseboards on his knees, taking care of his possessions. He was at his happiest when he was cleaning; it was meditative for him—certainly easier than sitting next to Ashley and sharing his most intimate thoughts and feelings. On Saturday night, they would go out and drink. Later they would fight about her choice in clothes and carefree barroom dancing.

Ashley was nervous about meeting Father Steve. Although she was not religious, she had attended Catholic schools while growing up and equated meeting Steve with meeting God. She was afraid he would see through her—her guilt about her failing marriage, her distance from the light. Upon sitting down, she barely looked at him, yet she was struck by his eyes—eyes that were full of emotion—eyes that knew her. As Steve asked her a few intuitive questions, Ashley knew she could no longer hide behind her playful sense of humor. Her game was over.

Ashley felt vulnerable talking to Steve, fearing that he was peering into her soul, even though his approach was nonthreatening, his voice soft and reassuring. As she began to open up and to share her feelings of guilt and her desire to get more out of her marriage, the tears began to flow.

On paper, Ashley's husband was a great guy. He worked hard as a manager, often putting in seventy to eighty hours a week; he took pride in his house, always helping to clean; and as far as she knew, he didn't fool around. There were, however, significant marital issues.

David's long hours on the job left little time for companionship, his heavy drinking bordered on alcohol dependency, and he did not show much interest in trying to take their lives to a higher, more meaningful level; his focus seemed to be on acquiring nice things, obtaining financial security, and enjoying his beer and his friends. He would set guidelines for Ashley's dress and behavior, telling her what was and was not acceptable—and when they were intimate, he was rough, at times hurting her.

Ashley felt like a failure. She thought she was asking for more than she deserved, that she alone was responsible for her marital problems. She also drank excessively, worked long hours, and spent little time looking inward.

Over the course of the lunch, Ashley noticed how gently Father Steve was "lifting the rock"—the rock she lay hidden beneath, the one that offered her protection. As she came to better understand her role in the marriage, she came to understand the truth of her life—her flirtatious behavior that came out of loneliness, the absence of spiritual peace in her life, her newfound desire to find meaning. These revelations came through Steve's simple but intuitive questions, eventually leading her to face the difficulties of her childhood—a father and stepfather who drank heavily and beat her, a mother who was untrusting of outsiders and afraid to show affection, a grandmother who treated her like a street beggar. She also came to understand how her life experiences had enabled her to become a people pleaser, someone who craved attention and affection, someone who chose to avoid the pain of past hurts by focusing on humor and lightheartedness.

On reflection, Ashley realized that Father Steve hadn't provided any answers during their lunch. In fact, he had asked very few questions. His caring presence had simply allowed her to release her fears, to recognize that her focus needed to begin with herself. She would start her life anew, making choices from strength and with clarity of vision. Father Steve had opened a door, and now she would walk through it.

Why do we fear?

Such an innocent question. One asked by Jesus himself, along with many other people. I think each of us hopes for a simple answer, an instruction on how to avoid fear.

We fear what we feel we can't control is the simplest answer I can provide. Once we identify our fear, removing it is as simple as understanding it.

—David Sifri, a spiritual communication

Through the eyes of beauty
The world unfolds with love

CHAPTER 13

Fear Is an Opportunity

When I was in the latter years of my practice, I would occasionally invite patients who were in need of more time back to my office where they would encounter a room alit with candles, a multitude of tropical plants and trees, the sound of water trickling down a five-foot slate fountain, and the faint but sweet smell of simmering vanilla. As they sank into a large brown leather chair, they would find themselves surrounded by glass crosses and wooden angels, a large photograph of a soaring eagle, a life-size replica of a brownish-orange sea turtle, and spiritual knickknacks from various ethnic and religious cultures. A rotating prism hung in the window transforming sunshine into light-filled rainbows that slowly encircled the room. Outside, mourning doves rested in a feeding basin while brownish-red sparrows busily devoured sunflower seeds.

As my patients got comfortable, I would often tell them about the solar-powered chimes that reminded my guests of truths that were expressed—as they rang spontaneously but precisely at the end of meaningful thoughts and statements put forth by anyone in the room. My patients were often skeptical upon hearing this. When they questioned me, I assured them that it was true—the chimes were interactive. I went on to tell them that many times when someone had recently passed, the chimes would go crazy, as if to say "I am here" in a most beautiful and harmonic manner—often bringing forth a smile or tear to my visitors.

❦

Sharon came to see me because she was finding it difficult to sleep, experiencing panic attacks, and having suicidal thoughts. There was a reluctance on her part to share her feelings of sadness with anyone; even her husband was unaware.

Upon entering my office, Sharon was taken aback. The thirty-odd plants, soft-lit candles, and flowing water caught her by surprise. She was momentarily uplifted as the energy soothed and comforted her. Her face softened into a smile.

During her visit, Sharon told me she felt overwhelmed by her new job and her life in general. Aside from the stress at work, communication with her husband was limited, and she felt her life lacked purpose. She spoke of having constant worries and self-doubt. She alluded to past hurts and to subsequent counseling, which had never been beneficial.

We began by talking about the need for her to quiet the noise in her life, to let go of the fear and re-center herself with love. As I watched Sharon, I could tell the words were resonating with her. She was remembering past experiences when she had felt love in her heart, times in church when she felt close to God. She realized that it was time for her to reconnect—to release pain and embrace light, to look for a deeper meaning in her life. Sharon left my office that first day with the intention of starting to read more spiritual material and to focus on the joyful things in her life. Prayer would be helpful. She would also start taking an antidepressant medication.

Over the next couple of visits, Sharon appeared to be doing better. She stated that she was feeling more empowered and spiritually connected. During her fourth visit, however, she seemed to have taken two steps backwards.

Sharon had recently lost her father, and as we sat and talked, she disclosed that he had sexually abused her. The abuse started at the age of eight and continued throughout her teenage years. I asked her if she felt guilty about what had happened. She told me she had never done anything to stop her father's advances because she was afraid of how he might react. Sharon went on to tell me that her father, for undisclosed reasons, stopped speaking to her on the day of her wedding. She hadn't spoken to him since; it had been six years.

Watching Sharon, I knew her energy was at an all-time low. It was clear to me that she was seeing herself as a victim, weak and powerless. As she sat slumped in the leather chair, I noticed her eyes were moist. She was ready to give up. She had many questions—angry questions. Wasn't it enough that God had taken her mother from her at the age of three? Why had God given her a sexually abusive father? Why had her father stopped speaking to her on the day of her marriage, a day that was supposed to be celebratory? Why hadn't God played a more protective role in her life?

I explained to Sharon that God had always been with her—walking with her and sharing her pain. When I told her this, the solar-powered chimes sounded. I took her hand and let her know that there wasn't anything positive in seeing herself as a victim. I went on to explain that viewing herself in that way disempowered her, causing her to feel helpless. As I said this, I held my hand so that it was just barely off the floor. I told her this was the energy of a victim—very low. The chimes rang lightly, once again. I suggested that spirituality was always about empowerment—about seeing yourself up high. As I spoke, I moved my hand upward, close to the ceiling. Again, the chimes went off. By now, the chimes were starting to bring a smile to Sharon's face. She understood that something greater was happening, that someone was listening. Spiritual love was with her, trying to guide and comfort her, to remind her of her beauty within.

We went on to discuss the need for Sharon to face her fears, to stop hiding. The chimes emitted a soothing sound. I could tell her energy was rising. Her posture became more upright. I asked her if she had ever directly addressed her father's abuse. She told me she had recently discussed it with some of her siblings, but they did not share her perspective. They were more inclined to sweep the unpleasant events under the rug. Some of them, too, had been abused.

I explained to Sharon that I did not believe it was by accident that she had chosen me as her physician; spirit had brought us together. She had sought out someone who would help her address her fears. On some level, she was ready to deal with her past.

I suggested that it was time for her to confront her father, to speak her truth. Even though her father was no longer of this world, he would hear her words. The chimes resonated softly. I went on to say that I thought it would be easier for her to address the abuse now, since her communication with her father would not be face-to-face, and added that as she expressed her feelings and thoughts, and sent herself love, healing would occur. The chimes rang sweetly. Sharon said that she might begin by writing him a letter.

We went on to talk about how it was important to look for the opportunity within her experience—to see the beauty in it. The beauty would come with insight, with the chance to learn more about forgiveness, empathy, empowerment, and love—love that always began inwardly with gentleness. Once she came to embrace these opportunities, she could emerge from the experience with greater strength and appreciation; she could transform this unpleasant happening into something meaningful. There would be growth, understanding, and enlightenment. The chimes tolled gently.

When I expressed my desire to share her story with others, Sharon said that would be wonderful. She told me it would be one more opportunity to turn the experience into something meaningful, hopefully by helping others. Once more, the chimes rang.

As Sharon looked into my eyes, she said that for the first time in her life she felt ready to shed light upon what happened, to deal with the issues head-on and to stop hiding. She paused for a moment and then, as the chimes sounded, smiled. She had been waiting for them, for their confirmation. She knew that it was time for her to face her fears, time for her to live.

Upon leaving my office that day, Sharon appeared transformed—energized, purposeful, and radiant. She was remembering who she was—not a victim but an empowered, beautiful, spiritual being.

When I saw Sharon several weeks later, she appeared lighter, more alive. The heaviness that had draped her like a thick winter coat had been shed. As she waited in my office, I asked her to read a rough draft of her story. On my return, she told me she felt the story was accurate. When I looked down at the pages, I noticed she had scribbled something in the margins. She had written the word "chimes"—which had sounded as she read certain passages. She had marked those passages with parentheses. Spiritual love was with her, trying to guide her and comfort her, to remind her of her beauty within—chimes. There would be growth, understanding, and enlightenment—chimes. It was time for her to begin her life anew—chimes. As I read the marked passages, I felt overwhelmed. This beautiful force never ceased to amaze me—so kind, so gentle, so loving, so ever-encouraging.

Talking with Sharon, I learned that she had begun writing a long letter to her father. As she wrote, crying continuously, her anger and pain poured forth onto the pages. There weren't enough words to express how she felt. She was relieving stress that had built up over fifty years and refused to hold anything back.

Through this process, Sharon had gradually come to understand that her father had been a miserable person. He had been left with four children when her mother died. Shortly thereafter, he had re-married out of convenience rather than love.

In time, Sharon had come to do everything for her father—all of his cooking, shopping, and laundry. Although he was capable of taking care of himself, she had become his personal valet. On entering the third decade of her life, however, she had decided to marry. Her husband was gentle and spiritual, but her father, who was an atheist, had little tolerance for a man of such ideals … so he had become quiet, expressing his displeasure through silence.

Sharon was not yet ready to forgive her father; however, she was beginning to understand. She was different now—spirit was with her in a way she had never dreamed possible. She felt comforted and guided, cared for and loved. The chimes had spoken to her in a man-ner she could never have imagined.

Sharon began nurturing the little girl inside of herself as she prepared to soar. Tears ran down her face as she spoke of her appre-ciation for her newfound joy in life, rich with potential and love. She no longer saw herself as a victim; fear had become an opportunity.

Graciously accept what life brings forth
By quieting your everyday fears
And trusting in divine love

CHAPTER 14

We Quiet Our Fears through Trust

I asked Matthew, a patient of mine who had suffered a life-changing back injury years ago, if he felt the accident was in some way meaningful to him.

Without hesitation, he replied, "Definitely!"

Matthew struggles to rise from a chair, walks using a cane, has uncomfortable back spasms throughout the day and night, and has difficulty controlling his movements. He also finds it mentally challenging to deal with his discomfort and his limitations. Yet his experience has awakened him to the graciousness of others—to their willingness to reach out and touch, to make a difference in his life.

Although a caring individual before the accident, Matthew feels that since he was injured he has become more empathetic toward people struggling with physical and emotional disabilities, openly sharing his thoughts and experiences with them when he thinks it might be beneficial.

His greatest pleasure comes from helping others. He enjoys extending simple acts of kindness, such as holding open a door at church, and is amazed at how appreciative people can be as they extend a smile and a thank you.

Matthew attends religious services regularly. He has become more spiritual since the accident, which he says brought him back to God. Before his injury, Matthew drank heavily; now he abstains.

Although Matthew has struggled continuously since the accident, he harbors no resentment. He tries not to wallow in self-pity, but when he does feel down, he pushes himself to get out of the house and to interact with others, after which he usually feels better. This isn't to say that Matthew finds it easy to deal with it all, but he strives to move forward in spite of his severe limitations. One of his proudest achievements was finishing a demanding physical-rehabilitation course. The pride he derived from this accomplishment arose from the courage and perseverance he discovered within.

Rather than resisting the changes that have taken place in his life, Matthew has embraced them. He has reconnected with spiritual love through trust. This man who is continually challenged by his injuries has found that his greatest joy comes not from focusing on himself but from helping others ... from the shared intimacy of "a smile and a thank you."

I asked Rylan, a kindhearted, charismatic eighteen-year-old server, if he agreed with the following statement ... "Love knows no boundaries."

"Absolutely!" he exclaimed.

"Why do you believe that?" I inquired with genuine curiosity.

"Because love is all about acceptance ...
About seeing people for who they are."

CHAPTER 15

Does God Judge?

Many of us are taught from an early age that God judges everything we do. But why would God do that? Judgment creates fear. I would suggest that since God is love, and love always looks for the best in everything, there is no need for such judgment. Love is simply appreciation—like seeing the beauty in a flower.

While I believe that God does not judge, I am not suggesting that our thoughts, words, and actions are without consequence. When we act in ways that are not true to ourselves, we create more disharmony within and move further away from peace. Yet none of us exhibit perfect loving actions all of the time, nor, in my opinion, are we meant to. We are here to learn and to grow—to commune with the divine and to celebrate our being.

If love does not judge, then each of us might ask ourselves ...
"Am I capable of learning not to judge?"

This, however, is not an easy task. We are so used to judging others that it takes considerable effort not to do so. We haven't experienced what others have experienced; nor do we know their individual paths.

Yet when we let go of judgment and reconnect with love, we are able to reach out to those in need—to those who are struggling—with empathy, compassion, and understanding. Rather than being critical of others and causing them to feel unworthy, we are able to remind them of who they are … spiritual beings on a human journey. We become open to their teachings, to their beauty, to their piece of God's puzzle. We foster feelings of oneness and harmony, of hope and empowerment.

A number of years ago, I decided to emulate this philosophy with my children. Rather than criticizing them for inappropriate behavior, I chose to simply communicate my concerns in a more peaceful and engaging manner. Although it required greater patience and a more loving state of mind, the result was a more positive experience for everyone.

As my children grew, I tried to focus solely on their inner beauty. It seemed to me that the more beauty I could see in them, the more beauty they were able to see in themselves. Even if my children faltered, as we all do, I tried to keep my emphasis on their true nature—a spiritual nature of love, purity, and light. As a parent, my greatest joy comes from stroking my children's faces, sharing humor with them, gently guiding them with love and respect, and listening to their insights and life experiences with wonder and appreciation—understanding that in the end they must walk their own path, that they are my greatest teachers, and that the most I can offer them is a reflection of their own beauty in my eyes.

As we come to understand that there is no need to judge others, we begin to experience true unconditional love. We no longer feel inclined to withhold love from those who at one time we might have deemed unworthy, nor do we have the inclination to withhold love from ourselves, for we have come to understand that everyone is deserving.

❧

Andy is thirty-seven years old. He has short blond hair and a smile that can light up a room. He's of medium height and athletically built, but his eyes are his most telling feature. They're inviting eyes— eyes that sparkle with excitement, reflecting the beauty and energy of life. His is a story of how he found love in a setting of darkness, of how he found God amid the chaos of fear.

Throughout his life Andy has struggled with self-love, frequently feeling he was not good enough, feeling less than whole. Unfortunately, the religious teachings to which he was subjected only made him feel worse, like a sinner—someone unclean. Although Andy attended church regularly while he was growing up, he found it boring. He wanted to do other things, to put on his blue jeans and play outside.

Because of these feelings, Andy thought he was a bad kid. The lessons he learned in church only made him feel worse. The sermons stressed that if you were bad, you were going to hell. These dire warnings caused Andy to lie in bed at night in absolute terror, thinking about hell—"a place where the most horrible things would happen to you for all of eternity, a place where you were tortured forever and ever, a place where the torture was fresh every time." As Andy thought about it, he concluded, "God can't be that nice!"

Andy was yelled at often as a kid. He had a contentious relationship with his mother, and his father, whom he feared, worked long hours. He also fought frequently with his sister. It was not unusual for Andy to get mad at both parents and think about how much happier he would be if they weren't around.

When Andy was six years old, his parents gave him a jersey at a sports banquet. Even though he wasn't on the team, his parents offered it to him to help him feel included. Andy thought it was the "ugliest thing ever made." The next day in his first-grade classroom, Andy started crying. He felt guilty. He knew his parents had given him the shirt out of consideration, yet he thought it was "crap." It didn't seem possible for him to be honest with himself, to acknowledge his true feelings about the shirt, and still feel good about himself.

At the age of eight, Andy's cousin Jodi and her family came to visit. Jodi was attractive and eight years older than Andy. Andy had always loved women, and when they were alone together, he asked Jodi if she would show him her "boobs." Jodi was horrified. She ran upstairs and told the whole family—his aunt and uncle, his mom and dad, and his grandmother—what had happened. Andy's father came downstairs and told Andy how much he had embarrassed them. Andy was ticked off. He couldn't believe Jodi had reacted that way. He was just sexually curious, but because of his interest in his cousin's body, his family inferred that there was something wrong with him.

At the next family gathering, Andy called Jodi downstairs. She was barefoot, and unbeknownst to her, Andy had placed a tack on one of the steps. As Jodi came down the stairs, she stepped on the tack. While she was crying in pain, Andy thought to himself, *That's what you get.* Later, however, came the feelings of guilt—the remorse and self-doubt.

At age twelve, Andy began to listen to the heavy-metal band Iron Maiden, in particular the song "Number of the Beast" from the album of the same name. Andy thought the music was cool. The song was actually based on the dream of a band member. The lyrics, which included "666—the number of the beast," didn't seem that dark to him even though the band was singing about the devil. Over time, however, Andy began to have "crazy thoughts"—"flashes of people being beaten, violent bloody thoughts." These thoughts came to him even though Andy had never been a violent person.

As a youth, Andy had been an excellent diver, performing triple front flips and double gainers without difficulty; but after he started listening to heavy-metal music, he began to have difficulty performing dives that used to be easy for him. He would have "bad thoughts" before going off the diving board and would lose his focus, often injuring himself in the process.

During his teenage years, Andy's grandma told him to ask Jesus to touch his heart. She went on to say that if he did so, he "would get this warm feeling all over." Although Andy tried to follow her advice, the feeling he got was not sufficient enough to help him overcome his fear of hell, to overcome his feelings of nonacceptance and inadequacy.

Upon entering college, Andy was "antireligion and anti-Christian." He describes this phase as his "dark period." As he put it, "nothing had any meaning." During this time, Andy used a lot of recreational drugs, including LSD and mushrooms. The drugs led to some unpleasant experiences, some of which caused him to believe he was in hell—a hell reminiscent of his earlier church years, complete with monsters and demons.

While in college, Andy eventually came to the realization that his life was going in the wrong direction. His boyhood optimism, which had never been great, was fading. It was as if he had lost a piece of his soul, a piece that would not be easily retrievable. For a long time, Andy had felt that "a part of me is gone," a part that was more loving and forgiving. What had replaced it was something darker and more judgmental.

Andy began to look for a way out. In an effort to address his problem, he decided to tell his father about his drug use, but when he spoke of his experiences with LSD, his father reacted with disappointment and grew visibly upset. Andy had hoped to find an extended hand from his father but instead found judgment and condemnation. The message Andy heard was that he had fallen short, that his actions were not those of an upright moral being. Yet he felt that he had broken a barrier with his father—a line of communication had been established. From then on, their relationship was defined by honesty. Over time, Andy's father became his best friend.

Andy eventually met a girl who saw him for who he was. Jenna was the first person with whom he felt he could really open up. An intelligent girl, she often asked deep, probing questions. There was no room for game playing with Jenna; she was too sharp. Andy had to be honest with her, but he felt no judgment from her as he shared his innermost thoughts and feelings. She was accepting of him despite his past, offering him love and understanding.

In time, Andy and Jenna's relationship flourished. As they began to anticipate a long-term future together, they found their way back to church. Although they were both more spiritual than religious, Jenna wanted to raise their children in a loving religious environment. She desired that their kids be baptized, and Andy agreed. They sought out a church that would focus on love rather than on sin and hell—one that would be different from the church of Andy's childhood.

One Sunday at church, Andy was praying for a sick friend of his named Robert. As he prayed for Robert to find comfort and healing, Andy had an unusual experience. In what appeared to be a glimpse of the future, he saw Robert, shortly after his death, kneeling before Christ and looking up, his eyes wide open. While he continued to watch, Andy noticed that Jesus appeared just as he had always envisioned, except that he radiated a bright rectangular light from his upper nose and eyes. Andy could feel the total calm, peace, and joy emanating from Jesus as Robert gazed up at him.

Andy realized that Jesus knew everything about Robert and that Robert was seeing the entire truth of himself and his life—his actions that arose from love and his actions that arose from an absence of love. Yet this took place in a setting of complete understanding and acceptance. There were no distractions—no judgment, no fear—only truth and the purity of light. Robert was learning about life in the most powerful manner possible—through the gentle, inspiring, and unending love of Christ.

During another Sunday service, Andy had a similar vision, only this time he glimpsed his parents' experience at death, as they met Jesus in a manner similar to Robert's. When Andy witnessed this, he knew he was peering into the unknown. He also knew with certainty that this was how it would be at the end of his life; he would experience comfort, healing, and immeasurable love and light. As Andy reflected on this, he came to understand that life is short, that none of us are here for long. He also realized that for the first time in his life he felt the total absence of fear, total relief from the anxiety of life.

Andy wanted to cry from the awe-inspiring beauty he'd observed during these end-of-life visions. He had never been one to embrace the "lovely stuff"; he had always seen it as a sign of weakness. Now he thought differently. Andy understood that the challenges of life were something you had to work through, that age and experience were helpful. He also understood that life is a work in progress, that he simply needed to do the best he could in a setting of self-awareness and honesty. In the end, it was all about love, about coming to see the beauty in everyone ... about coming to see the beauty in himself.

PART IV

Peace through Love

I take care of my inner child. It is the child who is frightened. It is the child who is hurting. It is the child who does not know what to do. I will be there for my child. I embrace it and love it and do what I can to take care of its needs. I make sure to let my inner child know that no matter what happens, I will always be there for it. I will never turn away or run away. I will always love this child.

—Louise L. Hay, *Letters to Louise*

CHAPTER 16

We Must Learn to Love Ourselves

Angela, a twenty-eight-year-old nursing student who suffers from depression, was physically abused by her father throughout her childhood. She recalls one episode when her parents were arguing in their station wagon during a family vacation. After her father stopped the car, her parents stepped outside to settle their disagreement. When her mother climbed back into the station wagon, she had a fat, bloody lip. Her father then got back into the car, turned it around, and drove home.

When Angela was seven years old, she was play-wrestling with her father. As her father grabbed her hand, he crushed some potato chips she was holding. Thinking that Angela had crushed the potato chips on purpose, he threw her across the room, breaking her arm. True to form, he later apologized. He continued to be abusive until Angela was eighteen, when he gave her a black eye; she pressed charges and had him sent to jail.

Angela eventually forgave her father for his abusive behavior.

In a soft and loving voice, she told me she had learned to accept her father for who he was. She understood that he had not grown up in an environment that was conducive to learning caring behavior. The fact that he sought medical help for his violent temper and took steps to rectify his anger problem helped her to see his humanity.

I first met Angela, a nursing student, after she was hospitalized for attempting to commit suicide. Prior to her hospitalization, she had been repeatedly belittled by a nursing instructor during a clinical. Feeling angry and hurt, Angela had decided to walk off the nursing floor. Before she left the hospital, however, the instructor began taunting her again, asking why she was willing to throw away her nursing career over their unpleasant interactions. Unbeknownst to the instructor, Angela had reached a point in her life where she refused to tolerate any more physical or emotional abuse.

The instructor's words continued to echo in Angela's mind after she left the floor. The thought of letting down all the people who had helped her move toward her goal of becoming a nurse was painfully overwhelming. Angela felt she couldn't live with their presumed disappointment. After driving to a park, where she felt utterly alone, Angela swallowed all of her prescription medication.

When I saw Angela shortly after her hospitalization, she had been stripped of all her defenses. Like a butterfly freshly emerging from its cocoon, her protective covering had been discarded, revealing her innocence and purity. With her anguish muted, Angela was prepared to search for her inner light; she had been to the abyss and now with quiet hopefulness would learn to fly anew.

Angela spoke of her hospitalization, of the discomfort of having a nasogastric tube "put down" her nose so her stomach could be pumped. She remembered vomiting and having charcoal placed in her stomach to absorb the drugs on which she had overdosed. Her most anguishing memory, however, was of the realization that she might never again be able to stroke her children's faces or tenderly hold her husband.

Angela's focus was now changing—the winter coldness of despair transforming into warm seedlings of love.

Several months later, Angela reappeared in my office. She had been somewhat erratic about taking her antidepressant medicine and was still struggling with feelings of sadness and hopelessness. As we talked, I discovered that Angela had been sexually abused at a daycare center when she was eight years old. The woman who had abused her was now deceased, and Angela had never had the opportunity to confront her.

I explained to Angela that in the spiritual world communication was always possible. She could still converse with the woman who had abused her. By allowing herself to feel the emotions she had repressed and then expressing those emotions to her abuser through thought, spoken word, or written word—she would promote self-healing. As she continued to work through those emotions, she would ultimately be able to extend forgiveness. At the same time, it would be important to send herself light and love.

Before Angela left my office, I drew a heart on one of her wrists and had her draw a heart on the other one. I then encouraged her to send herself love whenever she looked at the hearts ... explaining that it is through love that healing occurs.

I saw Angela again several weeks later. She was doing better. She had begun to get in touch with her repressed feelings and was communicating those feelings to the woman who had abused her. For a one-week period, Angela had screamed at her abuser for the trauma she had caused—vocalizing the feelings of violation and dirtiness that still lingered within her.

By the end of the week, Angela had begun to feel calmer. Although she was still unable to extend forgiveness to her abuser, she was on the road to spiritual healing. At the same time, she had begun to send herself love—drawing small hearts on her inner wrist and allowing herself to feel good when someone complimented her on her nursing skills.

The next time I saw Angela, she was helping teenagers with disfiguring illnesses. These kids often had blistering skin diseases that limited their ability to interact closely with others. Many of these teens were wards of the state; their parents offered little family support since they frequently suffered from drug addictions and other maladies themselves. While Angela tended to these patients and changed their dressings, she heard their innermost desires. They needed a familiar face, and they yearned for the human touch. More than anything else, they wanted someone to care about them.

As Angela listened, she came to understand that her life was nowhere near as challenging as those of her patients. She started to look at things in a more positive light.

Julia, one of the Angela's favorite patients, had a surprisingly optimistic attitude in spite of her disabling illness. Julia was a jokester. Angela tried to spend as much time with her as she could, many hours of which were outside of her normal work schedule. She thought of Julia as her little girl—never mind that Julia was twenty and Angela was still in that decade of her life as well. Julia's own mother was addicted to drugs.

Julia was told by her doctors that she would be dying soon. Although on the surface she projected a positive attitude, underneath she was angry and scared. As Julia struggled with her emotions, Angela listened and encouraged her to express her feelings. Angela wanted her to know it was all right to be afraid. She reminded Julia that she had touched many lives and that if God were calling her home, it was for a reason.

Angela knew, however, that Julia wouldn't "go home" until she was ready. In the past, Angela had seen many nursing home patients wait until they had seen a loved one, or until they were alone, to die. "Julia won't die," she softly exclaimed, "until she has accomplished what she wants to accomplish. The will of a human being is so powerful!"

As I listened to Angela, I felt a tranquility and peacefulness resonate with her words. Angela's anger over her previous abusive experiences was dissipating. She was moving toward forgiveness. She found she could better understand Julia's anger because of her own past experiences; there seemed to be meaning in all of her life events. Angela still had her good and bad days, but she was healing—no longer seeing herself as a victim.

On a subsequent visit, I asked Angela about Julia. She told me that Julia had passed away but that she had held on until her mother had come to visit. When I asked her if Julia had accomplished what she had intended before she died, Angela told me that she felt Julia's purpose had been to help teach the nurses to look past her physical attributes and to extend love to her as a spiritual being. When Julia had first arrived, many of the nurses were reluctant to get close to her. They were bothered by her bad smell from a complicated infection, her blistering sores, and the absence of fingers, hair, and teeth. It was difficult for them to treat her as they would anyone else—they saw her as a disease. With time, however, their attitudes and perceptions changed. As Julia engaged in different activities, such as wheelchair races with Angela in which she would speed down the hallways in her nub-controlled electric chair, she won the hearts of the nurses who were previously unwilling or incapable of overlooking her infirmities.

When Julia died, it was hard for them to see her go. They had fallen in love.

Guilt reminds us
Of who we are not

CHAPTER 17
───────────────

Guilt Remembers

O ur ability to achieve our potential is often hampered by guilt. We tend to forget who we are and what great qualities each of us has. We forget how connected we are with each other and with spiritual love.

Guilt reminds us of things we've done in the past when we were spiritually disconnected. As we look back at these thoughts or actions, we feel ashamed or embarrassed. The fact that we feel uncomfortable shows us that these thoughts and actions do not reflect our true nature. Instead of realizing that this behavior is foreign to our essence as loving, spiritual beings, we fear that it reflects our true selves. We start feeling very low because we're left with a vision of ourselves that is less than complimentary.

So what can we do? First, we can start by understanding that these thoughts and actions do not reflect our true spiritual nature—a nature of love, joy, and peace. Secondly, we can *embrace* these past experiences. Such experiences give us the chance to learn, to grow, and to create ourselves anew. They also give us the opportunity to extend a nonjudgmental hand to ourselves—to lift ourselves up through the gentleness of love.

☙

Within the last few years, Sarah lost both of her parents. Her father passed away first while he was in a nursing home. Although

Sarah had visited him daily at the facility, she couldn't be reached on the night he died because her phone had been accidentally left off the hook. In the days and weeks that followed, Sarah was distressed that she hadn't been able to comfort him in his final hours.

Sarah's mother died two years later. She had been residing in an independent-living complex affiliated with a nursing home. Two weeks before Thanksgiving, she suffered a fall. Shortly thereafter, a nurse from the facility contacted Sarah, informed her of the incident, and assured her that her mother was fine. Sarah continued to phone her mother on a daily basis but didn't actually visit her because she was preparing for the family's Thanksgiving gathering.

Four days before Thanksgiving, Sarah called her mother in the evening, but when there was no answer, she assumed she had gone to bed early and decided to call again the next morning. When there was still no answer the next day, she went to her apartment. As Sarah stepped out of the elevator, she saw her mother's newspaper in front of her door. She felt a sense of dread that only intensified when she discovered the door was unlocked. Upon entering the apartment, she found her mother dead in the foyer. Sarah was devastated.

Although the cause of her mother's death remains unclear, Sarah wonders whether she would have noticed anything unusual in her behavior if she had taken the time to visit her. She also feels guilty for not having spent more time with her during her final days.

When Sarah and I talked two years later, she still couldn't discuss what happened without becoming emotional. This caring, loving daughter continues to feel profound guilt over both of her parents' deaths even though she provided unending support throughout their lives.

☙

We frequently feel tremendous guilt and responsibility for what happens to our loved ones. Because of our deep love for them, we tend to think we never did enough to show the extent of that love. We focus on the love and care we didn't give rather than on all the love and care we did give. All too often we seem to look for the worst in ourselves.

Yet if we allow ourselves to celebrate our loving nature, we can experience peace within. Spiritual peace comes not from expecting perfection in ourselves and others but from appreciating the depth of love that resides within each one of us.

ॐ

For years David struggled with alcohol. He could curb his drinking for a while but would eventually falter. He had glimpses of achieving something greater with his life, of touching others in a meaningful way, but he felt he carried too much baggage from the past. He believed his education was too limited, and he viewed himself as one of the boys—a fun-loving, heavy-drinking kind of guy.

David sensed a greater calling. He wanted to become a spiritual leader, to show others the light, but for every step forward he felt that he took two steps back.

David's drinking was worse in times of stress. The guilt he felt after a binge only lowered his self esteem, robbing him of feelings of self-worth and self-love. This, of course, led to more drinking, which led to more stress and a worsening of his interpersonal relationships. During these periods, David became depressed. He was left feeling hopeless and alone, cursed by alcohol and unable to break free. While others watched him sink, they seemed to lose faith in him. This confirmed his worst fear, that he was destined to be "a drunk."

As a result, David was consumed by guilt. On occasion he tried to channel his thoughts of self-doubt into prayers asking for the spiritual strength to overcome the urges that eroded his self-control. When he did so, his prayers allowed him to be truer to himself, to let go of the guilt and unworthiness—but eventually he would spiral downward again, turning to alcohol for solace.

One night, after drinking heavily, David staggered to his van and went for a drive. He found himself lumbering down a familiar road—a miserable old street that reminded him of how little things had changed in his life. He knew that he was drunk and "needed to get the hell off the road." Just then, he saw his church, with its brightly lit cross, up ahead. Like a beacon of light, it was calling him home.

David veered into the church parking lot, ran his van up on the lawn, and finally came to a stop underneath the cross, his car buried deep in the church shrubbery. As dusk turned to night, he placed his head on the steering wheel and began to pray.

Within minutes, he heard a knock on the window and raised his head. Outside the van stood a half-dozen parishioners, all of whom knew David. They had just finished a church meeting and were wondering what was going on.

As the parishioners began talking with David, they realized he was drunk. They angrily demanded that he get out of the van.

David became belligerent and told them to leave him alone.

"One way or another, you're getting out of that van!" one of the them proclaimed as they continued to express their disappointment with his careless and inappropriate behavior while at the same time telling him he was capable of so much more. Finally, they called his wife to come and pick him up.

That night and the following day, David's wife communicated a loud and clear message: "Get your life together, limit the alcohol, or I'm leaving!"

As David drove back into that same parking lot the following Sunday and recalled what had happened there just days earlier, he became filled with apprehension.

Upon entering the church, he felt himself stiffen. The very same people who had previously berated him were now standing within twenty feet of the door.

As they neared him, however, he was struck by the tenderness in their voices, the warmth in their greetings. There was no fear, no condemnation, only the expression of love—a genuine blessing of invitation—from these parishioners in this place of peace and worship.

Like a child being cradled, David basked in their affection. He was reminded of a picture of Jesus, as he hung on the cross, inviting the criminal on his right to join him in paradise. Amid his own suffering, Jesus was filled with love and compassion for the repentant man.

David would remember that experience often, that wonderful feeling of love the church members had extended to him. It was a feeling he would cherish forever, one that would keep him moving forward in the most difficult of times.

Soon thereafter, David started to turn the corner; he enrolled in classes and cut back on his drinking. During difficult times, he continued to appeal to God for help, which comforted him and allowed him to reconnect with grace and understanding. This in turn gave him a more positive perspective and helped him to ward off the guilt and hopelessness that arose from his fear-based thoughts of failure.

In time David achieved his dream of becoming a spiritual leader. He now speaks with appreciation of those who helped him along the way, of those who expressed faith in him with loving kindness. He also revels in God's unending patience, of that gentle hand forever extended.

Her love is immeasurable
Except for herself

CHAPTER 18

True Love Begins with Self-Love

B etty, a frail elderly patient with gray hair and a smoker's voice, is scared that when she dies she won't go to heaven. She has emphysema and struggles to breathe—her closest companion being an oxygen tank. There are times, however, when even the mobile oxygen does little to help her short-windedness. During those instances, her anxiety becomes her worst enemy. As her mind races and panic ensues, she feels like she is suffocating.

When she was younger, Betty loved nursing and thrived on helping others. Her energy would surge as she walked into the hospital, reaching out to anyone in need, but she was unable to offer that same gentleness and affection to herself. It was reserved for her patients, her children, and her grandchildren.

Betty's strict parents didn't openly express their love for her as she was growing up. Although they provided for her material needs and tried to teach her right from wrong, Betty never experienced that tender human touch and, as a result, never developed any feelings of true self-worth. She went on to marry an alcoholic who, likewise, wasn't nurturing.

Betty recalls once telling a priest that, as a mother, she felt she could benefit from showing more patience toward her children. He responded by saying, "That is why there are so few mothers in heaven."

Such experiences merely reinforced her feeling that God's love was conditional, that she was unworthy.

ༀ

All of us, at times, may feel that we are unworthy of love, but as we come to experience spiritual love, we find ourselves immersed in its depth and gentleness. It is a love without judgment and fear ... a love rich with empathy, appreciation, beauty, and tenderness.

ༀ

An acquaintance of mine, Evan, grew up in a household with almost no demonstrative expressions of love. He was seldom if ever hugged and never heard his parents tell him they loved him. As he grew older, Evan struggled with feelings of sadness and emptiness. During these times, he would shut his mind off to the outside world and sleep ... thereby escaping the crippling feelings of hollowness and worthlessness.

At the age of nineteen, Evan confided in his girlfriend, Adria, that he had never told his parents he loved them, nor had they ever expressed their love for him. As Evan and Adria talked, she encouraged him to tell his mother how he felt. After about an hour, with Adria's persistent encouragement, Evan finally summoned the courage to do just that.

While Evan's mother was reading a book, Evan walked up to her hesitantly and said, "Hey, Mom."

"Yeah?"

"I just wanted to tell you ... I love you."

"Is Adria pregnant?" she asked.

"No," he answered, and trudged away, his heart filled with a deep ache.

Three years later, Evan and Adria were married. After another five years, their son, Charlie, was born. Although Evan's parents loved their new grandson, they did not show him much affection in the early months. Gradually, they became more loving and warm toward Charlie, but they still never expressed, or outwardly displayed, their love for Evan.

As Evan watched his parents' interactions with Charlie, he became jealous, angry, and filled with conflicting emotions, yet he never blamed Charlie for his feelings. More than anything, he was just confused. He wondered why they were so willing to express their love for his son but not for him. During this same period of time, his marriage to Adria was crumbling.

Evan finally approached his parents and, in a voice choked with emotion, expressed the concerns that had bothered him for so long. His parents were caught completely off guard by his revelations. They had no idea he had been carrying such a burden all those years. Their hearts went out to him, and they tried to comfort him.

As Evan talked with his parents, he came to discover that they, too, had grown up in households devoid of any outward signs of parental love. His mom and dad had become affectionate with Charlie only after watching Evan's wife hug, kiss, and express her constant love for the baby. Despite their best intentions, they had never broken that barrier with Evan. The pattern had become too ingrained.

Although Evan has struggled with depression since childhood, his life has turned around as his parents have become more expressive with their love. They now give Evan hugs and tell him they love him every time they call or see him. His marriage and family have become stronger as he in turn has become more loving with his wife and son—as he has become more loving with himself.

Unkind thoughts, words, and actions
Arise when one is distant from the light

CHAPTER 19

The Unloving Actions of Others Are Not Personal

When people behave toward us in ways that are not spiritual or loving, we tend to take their actions personally. Such actions can be hard for us to accept. We are left asking ourselves ...

"Why did he treat me that way?"

"What did I do to deserve this?"

"Why doesn't she like me?"

Although on the surface these actions may seem to be aimed at us personally, they really aren't. They're merely a reflection of someone's spiritual state—perhaps someone's disconnection from a feeling of peace or oneness—or someone's inability to understand an event or situation.

I was at a gathering recently with a number of friends. Whenever one friend, Andrew, entered the room, I felt a strong negative energy emanating from him. It was an oppressive energy, one that caused the air in the room to become heavy and stale, almost suffocating. My natural reaction was to withdraw from him.

Andrew never said anything overtly negative, but his tone was cold and uninviting. Another friend of ours, Elizabeth, also found Andrew's behavior disturbing. In particular, she was bothered by some of his insensitive comments.

I realized after the gathering that Andrew was probably suffering from depression. I was therefore better able to understand his actions. Elizabeth, however, took Andrew's negative behavior personally. What she failed to understand was that his demeanor merely reflected his emotional state. When people are depressed, they are so internally focused that they often become oblivious to the negative impact their words or actions are having on others.

It is helpful for us to remember that when others use unkind words or exhibit unkind behaviors, it is a reflection of their own distance from the light. Their actions, arising from an unloving state of mind, can be difficult for us to accept though, since a part of *our* self-image is based on how we feel we are perceived by others. We *want* to feel loved and valued. If, however, we are able to resist taking these unloving words and actions personally, we are better able to stay centered—to understand and to radiate peace—to bring others back to love *through* love.

It is also important for us to realize that the words or actions we perceive as *unloving* may not be unloving at all. We may, at times, misunderstand or misinterpret another person's words, actions, or intentions based on our own fears and insecurities.

Whenever we feel that we are the recipients of the negative energy of another, it is helpful for us to stop and bless ourselves with love. Instead of relying on others to help us feel loved, we can send ourselves the love we feel we are missing. Our feelings of discomfort in these situations can serve as a valuable reminder: *let me love and bless myself as I would another, because I am worthy—because I am a spiritual being of the highest magnitude.*

In addition, it's beneficial to strengthen ourselves in such situations ... to remember it's about empowerment. We can create a bubble of peace, love, and harmony around ourselves—a bubble that helps to protect us from injury but is permeable. *Love* moves easily through its strong yet fragile walls, but *negative energy* cannot enter as freely because the great energy of love—the energy of spirit—is so concentrated within the bubble.

During these challenges, it's also important for us to look inward for answers.

Why?

Because God speaks to us through our hearts—for that is where our truth lies.

☙

Akeem is a physician from Pakistan. He is a soft-spoken Muslim who is actively involved with his mosque. As a Pakistani living in the United States, he occasionally encounters prejudice or intolerance, but even when faced with challenging circumstances, Akeem tries not to criticize or become defensive.

For several years, Akeem interacted closely with a fellow physician who was critical of him. This physician exhibited little awareness of his own insensitive behavior and was quick to erupt. Day in and day out, Akeem was subjected to his condescension and belittlement. His negativity toward Akeem, however, arose less from prejudice than from the frustrations he himself was facing in his own practice.

Eventually Akeem felt it necessary to remove himself from the situation. Despite the pain he suffered during that difficult period, Akeem never spoke poorly about the other physician. Even though frequently wounded by his colleague's comments and behavior, especially when he was tired or stressed, Akeem made every effort not to take such actions personally. Instead, he chose to feed forgiveness rather than anger, to extend love to someone who showed him little.

Akeem's greatest challenge of late hits closer to home. His faith is paramount to him—he holds it sacred, as a farmer does the soil. He has found raising his family while living in a Western culture, however, to be difficult. His children naturally identify more with Western values—independence of thought and a love of technology. So when his eldest son resists the family call to prayer and craves the comfort and companionship of a cellular phone, Akeem struggles on the deepest of levels.

Akeem was always the obedient son, the one who made his father proud. In turn, his father would do anything for him. He didn't demand; he asked. He didn't expect; he appreciated. So now Akeem finds himself in unfamiliar territory. He loves his children, and their happiness and well-being mean everything to him. He wants them to thrive in this new culture, but at the same time he yearns for them to appreciate and identify with their heritage—in particular, the beauty and richness of their faith.

In the aftermath of the 9/11 terrorist attacks, Akeem found himself being tested once again. One of his middle-aged patients told him she was not sure that she could continue to see him as her physician. She said that because of recent events she had difficulty trusting Muslims and thought maybe she should change doctors. When Akeem asked her why she was so distrustful of Muslims, she told him she had learned from watching television that all Muslims were terrorists. She went on to say that she believed the Islamic religion encouraged their radical behavior.

Akeem listened to her thoughtfully without getting upset or defensive and then quietly explained to her that what she'd heard was inaccurate. Islam, he told her, is love-based, and acts of violence against other people are not supported within the true Muslim faith. Akeem then talked about his values as a physician—his passion and dedication to care for his patients in the same way that he would care for his own family. As they talked, she came to better understand both Akeem and his Muslim faith. She continued to be his patient for many years.

I later asked Akeem if he had been upset or offended when his patient voiced such prejudice and fear. He told me he was more concerned with her misunderstanding his religion. As he spoke of wishing to increase his patient's understanding of his beliefs and of the love within his faith, I came to understand that Akeem truly did not take any of her comments personally. I realized that he was only looking at the situation through her eyes. With love in his heart, Akeem simply wanted to put her fears to rest.

Peering through a misty haze
One begins to see the beauty of the human soul

CHAPTER 20

When We Look for the Best in Others, We Find It

It amazes me how much our perceptions and attitudes influence our relationships with others. People who expect negative or positive interactions with others are seldom surprised. Why is this so?

Our negative or positive view of others affects our emotional state, which, in turn, affects our interactions with them. Our tone of speech, facial expressions, level of eye contact, and body posture all reflect our underlying feelings and affect the way others perceive us.

Another important factor that influences our interactions with others resides within our spiritual energy. When we act with an awareness of our oneness with God, we begin to appreciate our own underlying magnificence and the magnificence in others as well. When we seek the best in others within a setting of love and trust, we create a nurturing atmosphere that makes it more likely that they will look for the best in themselves—thereby connecting with their own spiritual energy. We have, in a sense, placed them in a loving environment in which their true beauty can shine. Or, put another way, our spiritual energy can ignite their spiritual energy. Take, for instance, a log placed next to another log that is burning brightly. The first log has the potential to burst into flames, and when it is exposed to an already burning log, this potential is realized.

※

Alexis loved playing soccer for her middle school. Although she was passionate about the sport, she also liked to joke around with her teammates and coach. She wanted the experience to be both fun and instructional.

Her soccer coach ran practices with a strict intensity. At times he was moody and would come across as intimidating. On a bad day, for example, he might limit water breaks despite long, hot practices. He wanted the players to know he was serious about soccer.

During the course of the season, Alexis started to feel as if the coach didn't like her. She thought he was singling her out too much— screaming at her when she made mistakes and giving her little positive reinforcement. Alexis figured the coach didn't appreciate her sense of humor and took her easygoing manner as a lack of commitment to the game. As the season progressed, her self-confidence suffered, and her enjoyment of the game began to wane.

By midseason, Alexis's parents noticed that she was becoming increasingly subdued and decided to discuss their concerns with her coach. They let go of their protective fears—that the coach disliked their daughter—and approached him in a positive and trusting manner. They told him that they knew he had Alexis's best interest at heart, and they appreciated his commitment to coaching but were concerned that Alexis was losing her confidence because she didn't feel that she was a valued member of the team.

Alexis's parents were both surprised and heartened when the coach said he was quite fond of Alexis and that he appreciated her sense of humor. He told them Alexis had many wonderful qualities and that he was committed to her having a positive experience. After their talk, he became more encouraging, and Alexis began having fun again.

Through this experience, Alexis's parents were reminded of how much beauty we can see in someone when we simply look for the best in that person—and how that person, in turn, can then see the beauty in another.

☙

I was in Chicago in the fall of 2003 for a medical-education course. In the past, whenever I had the opportunity to spend some time walking around the city, I would often purchase gift certificates from local restaurants and hand them out to homeless people. On this trip, I visited a fast-food establishment and bought a number of five-dollar vouchers.

As I strolled through the downtown area in the twilight of the early evening, I noticed a number of what I presumed to be homeless people lying against nearby buildings or soliciting donations. When I walked up to these people, I looked directly—and deeply—into their eyes. I wanted them to know that they were worthy of love and respect—that I saw them not as street beggars but as fellow human beings.

What amazed me was the gratitude and kindness each person showed me in return. All of them were so appreciative to have been given a coupon with which to buy a meal. Often, as I walked away, I would hear the words, "God bless you!"

I remember, in particular, one gentleman who was walking around in a daze. As I looked at him warmly and handed him a gift certificate, he awoke from his fog, smiled, and thanked me.

I will never forget how much joy I was given that night just by handing out some coupons to people in need of food. The experience reminded me of the beauty of the human spirit and how this beauty can be found even in the most challenging of circumstances. These wonderful street people openly expressed their love to me for simply sharing some bread. Later, as I reflected on the evening, I was reminded of how life's greatest gifts are often right in front of us.

CHAPTER 21

Reaching Out

As I meet with different people, I find it difficult to predict how a conversation will go. Some people who appear on the surface to be happy and outgoing become guarded, even defensive, during spiritual discussions, while others who seem shy or quiet become open and receptive. Naturally it is easier for me to connect with the latter. These connections leave me feeling high and energized, but every meeting, no matter how challenging, is surprisingly meaningful.

Oftentimes, during such challenging meetings, I find myself reaching out to people who have erected seemingly impregnable walls around themselves. And yet, when these barriers fall away, I experience breathtaking beauty … a vulnerable soul of love.

❦

I first met Lindsey, a drug rep in her twenties, when she made sales calls in my office. She struck me as a very spiritual person. She was always smiling and friendly. She appeared to be so happy and vivacious that I thought it would be interesting to learn what motivated her, so I asked her to lunch. I was already friends with two of her partners, and the three of us had shared many spiritual meals together. I thought that, perhaps, after having lunch with her, she might want to become a regular at our get-togethers.

Our lunch lasted about two hours that day, but from the beginning, our conversation was awkward. Lindsey didn't know me well, and I could tell she was uncomfortable. She would answer my questions, but her answers rang hollow on an emotional level. On the surface, it may have appeared that we were having a meaningful discussion, but on a deeper level, I felt something was lacking. The feeling of peace and joy that I normally experience when I am having a spiritual conversation with someone wasn't there, and I couldn't understand why. Toward the end of the meal, I said as much to Lindsey. She said she thought I was perceptive but didn't elaborate. I could tell she was ill at ease, and I left the restaurant feeling frustrated. I had come to the lunch to learn more about what motivated this young woman, and I left feeling as if I had tortured her for two hours.

Over the next few days as I reflected on our talk, I decided the challenge for me was to move past my feelings of frustration and to move forward with feelings of unconditional love and understanding for Lindsey. When I next saw her in the office, I told her I was sorry if my questions had made her uncomfortable, that sometimes things don't go as expected. As usual, she was kind and gracious.

A couple of weeks later, I saw Lindsey again and gave her a hand-made cross from Mexico—one that I had bought for her based on an intuitive feeling. She was appreciative and told me she knew exactly where she would place it in her new house. I was grateful that she was willing to maintain a friendship with me, despite our awkward beginning.

Several weeks after that initial lunch, Lindsey came to my office to thank me for taking the time to meet with her. She related that one of the topics brought up during our luncheon discussion caused her to realize that some unresolved family issues had been bothering her. She had since addressed those issues and was now feeling stronger. I was surprised and comforted by her kind words. She also told me that my personal questions about her spirituality had apparently left her in a "state of shock." She had come to understand that her traditional Catholic upbringing had left her with little room for independent thought. As she was growing up "everything was just expected," and she was never asked how she felt or what she thought about spirituality.

Since then I've had many more lunches with Lindsey and her partners. On one occasion, in particular, she greeted me with a warm hug. It was a hug that spoke of trust and love, one given freely and without reservation. I was touched. I felt that a transformation had taken place within her. Her barriers were down—her heart open.

About a year later, I again met with Lindsey and her partners for lunch. Although there was no specific agenda, I quickly came to realize that Lindsey was struggling physically and emotionally from injuries she had sustained in a motor vehicle accident. Her life had changed drastically after her car had been struck by a truck. She was experiencing tremendous pain from her neck, shoulder, and upper-back injuries, and medical science was providing few answers. Despite multiple medical visits, anti-inflammatory drugs, and many months of physical therapy, Lindsey was making little progress. This young woman, always so optimistic and vivacious, was finding it hard to maintain a positive attitude.

During the lunch, we all tried to lift Lindsey's spirits. I told her I thought she was facing a unique opportunity, explaining that when there doesn't appear to be a human solution to a problem, it is time to think spiritually. In these situations, it is as if a higher power is closing off other options to *encourage* us to look in a different direction—to seek other paths and to have the faith and courage to pursue them. Lindsey admitted that she had spent little time looking for a spiritual answer.

We decided to focus on love and its healing power. As a way for the four of us to express our mutual love, we each drew a small heart on our own wrist and on the wrists of everyone else, but our primary focus was on Lindsey—on sending her love. As we drew the hearts on Lindsey, I could feel her energy and awareness increase. Meanwhile, the feeling of love between the four of us was intensifying. It was as if an invisible energy was uniting us and raising us up. By the time we left the lunch, Lindsey was all smiles and back to her normal self.

The next day, I received a voice-mail message from Lindsey:

"Hi, George—it's Lindsey. I have to tell you the most amazing story about what happened today. First of all, thank you for lunch yesterday. I had a great time. You're not going to believe this story! I stopped in this cute little jewelry store that some of my girlfriends had told me about. The little girl in there was really, really helpful, very sweet. At the end, as we were signing out, she hands me the receipt, and I look at her wrist, and she's got a little pink heart tattooed on it. A tattoo that looks exactly like the hearts we drew on each other, except it was pink. I asked her about it, and she said her best friend and her have them because they have both been through a lot, but through everything they know they have had each other and their families, and it is a way to show each other love. I almost started crying. I was like 'Oh my God, you've got to be kidding!' So I told her the story of how it happened to us yesterday. And she was like, 'Yeah, that's exactly why we thought it was a really cool thing to do.'"

Lindsey ended by saying, "A simple, really cool, not even filled-in, little pink heart ... I thought you would enjoy that story. Thanks again for lunch. I will talk to you soon. Bye."

A short time later, I received another voice mail from Lindsey. She sounded excited as she related that, as her thinking had become more positive and focused on spiritual healing, she had met a holistic therapist and for the first time in a year was making significant progress. She felt most appreciative.

Spiritual conversations occasionally take us out of our comfort zone, even under the best of circumstances. I know that my initial unconventional discussions with Lindsey about a mystical spiritual universe left her feeling uncomfortable; yet her ability to radiate so much positive energy and kindness, and her willingness to courageously explore this unconventional topic, spoke to me of the great spiritual potential she had within.

Our greatest growth often takes place when we find ourselves in unfamiliar territory. As I continue to engage people spiritually, I hope to become more adept at putting them at ease. I realize, however, that God works in mysterious ways and that the discomfort some people feel may actually promote their spiritual development.

To simply appreciate
A child's smile
A gesture of love
And the purity of God

It was a Friday morning, and I had just arrived at the office. I was trying to light an orange-vanilla scented candle on my desk to no avail. The wick was very short, and even though I was using a butane lighter with a long neck, it wouldn't ignite. I held the flame to the wick for a long minute, melting the wax around it. Still, no luck. Upon closer look, I noticed the curling of previously melted orange wax near the top of the candle. It's soft-appearing texture was minutely rippled, giving the candle a vulnerable, almost lifelike appearance—a look of delicate beauty.

I wondered if holding the candle might make it easier to light. Was there something magical about the power of the human touch? I picked up the candle, as I might a cherished object, and tilted it on its side. When I held the flame to the almost imperceptible wick, the candle came to life. I couldn't help but think of the human analogy. Was it easier to reignite the light in others through the human touch? When we look at others closely, do we become more appreciative of their beauty? These thoughts reminded me of a story.

I met fourteen-year-old Felicia and her mother at a restaurant for dinner after her mother told me that Felicia, whom I had never met, was having emotional problems. She had recently gone through a traumatic experience and was now on psychiatric medication.

When I met Felicia, she was somewhat disheveled. She had been vomiting, and it was unclear whether this was caused by a gastrointestinal virus, her medication, or her nerves. In any event, she didn't look well.

Felicia was wearing a black T-shirt and pants. Her brown hair was of medium length, and her face was round, like that of a child. In fact, she reminded me of a lost and vulnerable little girl—an impression that was further cemented in my mind when she called her mother "Mommy," something I found endearing but telling.

As I watched Felicia, I noticed her attention seemed to be drifting constantly; she frequently zoned out with a blank look on her face. I was curious, although slightly apprehensive, about how the evening would unfold. I wanted to help Felicia, but I also knew I was relying mainly on my intuition. I was there to assist her, but I had no game plan. Nor did I consider myself a professional counselor. I was merely hoping to bring some spiritual light and peace into her life.

Shortly after we met, I gave Felicia a white fluffy bear with an attached box of specialty chocolates. I told her I found it interesting that the bear had a small tear in the seam of its arm. I went on to say that I had noticed the imperfection before I bought the bear, but rather than exchange it for a new one, I thought it would be more appropriate to give her this one. I suggested that the tear actually made the bear unique and, in some way, more appealing. Watching her face, I got my first glimpse of Felicia's warm and wonderful smile. She hugged the bear.

As her mother and I talked, Felicia's focus continued to waver. In an effort to engage her, I told her I had come to try to help her, but I was uncertain of how to do this. She listened, but I wasn't sure how much she was taking in, given her upset stomach and short attention span. Perhaps the most I could do was to plant a seed.

After talking briefly about spirituality, I asked Felicia if she could hand me the bear. I realized that this was the first time that I had held Felicia's attention for any length of time. I spoke to her about how the bear was beautiful despite its injury. The tear only reflected a past hurt to the bear; it didn't make it less lovable. I went on to say that throughout our lives we have all been injured in some way or another.

What was important was not our being perfect but our ability to heal our injuries.

I then asked Felicia what she could do to heal the bear. She pondered the question for a moment, then softly said, "Love it." I was surprised and touched by her response. For the short duration of our dinner, Felicia had appeared to be distracted and withdrawn, yet she had provided the perfect solution for the bear's problem.

I next asked her to draw a heart on her wrist, as I drew one on myself as well. Felicia was to send herself love every time she looked at it—just as she was to heal the bear with love. Once again, she flashed her sweet smile.

We quickly finished our meal as it became apparent that Felicia wouldn't last much longer. She wanted to go home. After dinner, I gave her mother a hug and wished Felicia a good night. I was caught off guard, and touched, when Felicia asked me for a hug as well.

A week later, I received a wonderful thank-you card from Felicia. It was decorated with a variety of hearts boldly accented with metallic flakes. On the inside of the card, Felicia expressed her appreciation for the bear and stated:

I didn't realize that things that aren't perfect can still be loved.

I was surprised once again at the love and insight within this beautiful girl, and my eyes began to moisten. I was reminded of the candle whose wick had lit so easily with the human touch—that human touch that sees the delicate beauty and wonderment in all of life.

C H A P T E R   2 2

Love Is Present in the Now

Amy, a twenty-two-year-old Italian American and recent college grad, worked in my office while undergoing a difficult pregnancy. By the fifth month of her pregnancy, her baby faced a number of health issues, possibly resulting from an underlying chromosomal abnormality. Amy was so distraught over her baby's future that she did little else but worry. Rather than enjoying the tiny life within her, this animated four-foot-ten-inch girl, with the face of an angel and the mouth of a sailor, was overcome with fear.

Whenever Amy shared her concerns with me, tears spilled down her face as she gave voice to those worries. There were no clear answers. Different doctors were saying different things. She didn't know whom or what to believe.

Gradually, though, as Amy talked with friends and family members, hope began to emerge. Sue, another one of our employees and the mother of a child with Down syndrome, was able to offer Amy a great deal of empathy and comfort. Her own twenty-two-year-old son, Chad, was the light of her life.

Amy delighted in the way Chad interacted with her during his visits to the office, his eyes sparkling as he playfully shouted "H-e-l-l-l-l-l-l-l-l-o, Amy!" and waited for her cheery "Hi, Chad!" in response. It was impossible not to fall in love with this grinning, affectionate young man who wanted only to feel that he belonged—that he was needed.

Eventually Amy came to understand that her real concern wasn't about giving birth to a child with a chromosome abnormality; it was her desire to have the typical experience of motherhood combined with her fear of what the future might hold for her unborn baby.

Over a period of weeks, Amy began to adopt a more spiritual perspective. She realized she wasn't as powerless as she had been feeling. She had a choice. She could continue to live in fear and obsess about her baby's uncertain future, or she could reach out to her little one in the most intimate of manners. By living in the present moment, she could fully embrace the tiny new life growing inside of her. She could enjoy the joy of motherhood and feel the spirit of God within this most precious being.

Amy started to spend more time bonding and talking with the baby and reveling in the happiness that encompassed her when she felt her little one move. In the process, she also grew closer to her husband, Tommy. She came to feel a new appreciation for Tommy's kind and supportive nature, particularly when he sang silly songs to the baby and helped to keep the mood light. Although challenges and fears remained, Amy found that by focusing on her profound love for her baby and her husband, she was able to feel a renewed zest for life.

Two months later, Amy's son, Jack, was born with Down syndrome. When Jack was four months old, I asked Amy how her life had been affected by the birth of her son. Her face immediately lit up with joy as she described an overwhelming feeling of love. "Jack has brought me peace," she said.

As I looked over at Jack, I immediately understood. I couldn't help but notice his sweet, loving presence—those trusting, unwavering eyes and that oh-so-happy-to-see-you toothless smile.

Amy now feels hopeful for the future. She doesn't worry about Jack anymore, knowing on some level that everything will be all right. Although Tommy still has concerns, she has been able to transfer some of her hope and peace to him. By focusing on the joy of her baby, Amy spends little time worrying about what lies ahead. Instead, she lives in the present moment with her smiling gift of light.

Concern for others
May best be expressed
Through loving feelings

Jessica recently shared some of her family difficulties with me. Her parents, whom she loves, fight constantly and express little appreciation for one another. When she visits them, she often leaves feeling miserable. Jessica is worried about them and would like to intervene, but she's not sure how to approach them. When she thinks about the two of them, she becomes sad and frustrated. She has, however, found it helpful to pray for them, which leaves her with a sense of peace.

Many of us face similar circumstances with our loved ones. People close to us often struggle with some life situation that is causing them to suffer. How can we help them? Aside from directly offering words of support and comforting gestures of love, what else can we do?

We often lose sight of the fact that our feelings of love and peace, as well as our feelings of fear and worry, are conveyed to and received by those close to us on some level. As an example, one evening, my sister who lives in Philadelphia was experiencing excruciating back pain. The pain was so intense that she was crying intermittently throughout the night. Early the next morning, my concerned mother, sensing my sister's anguish from hundreds of miles away, called to ask her what was wrong.

I would suggest that by quieting our minds and connecting with our peace within, we can transform our own fear-based thoughts of worry and distress into love-based feelings of strength and peace, which are then transmitted to those who we feel are struggling. Prayer, meditation, and stillness can be meaningful tools in bringing about such a transformation. As we connect with spirit and send out feelings of love to those we cherish, we move closer to the light—and cause them to move closer to the light as well.

If Jessica can reconnect with feelings of love when she catches herself worrying about her parents, she will begin to feel more at peace. By taking time to re-center herself, she will radiate feelings of comfort and love, rather than those of unease, to her parents.

On a more personal level, I have found this to be helpful whenever I am concerned about someone. By quieting my mind of noise and fear, I move into a more tranquil state and focus on sending feelings of love, hope, and peace to those who are struggling.

We can also send loving feelings to others when we find ourselves thinking about them for unknown reasons. At these times, we may be sensing their need for help during a difficult period. The power of such loving feelings is enormous; we just need to remember who we are … spiritual beings on a human journey.

PART V

Connecting with God

I see the trees bending in the wind. I can also see beyond the trees the clear blue sky. As I stroll through the damp grass the moist grass rubs against my skin. As I look up at the sky I see the sun. I have to squint because of its brightness. I can also feel the heat burying into my shirt until it touches my skin.

Right now I am sitting in a chair with the cool air around me. I am startled by the air conditioning popping on. The smell of flowers fills the air. I feel the dog's soft warm hair rubbing against my skin. I hear the birds whistling in the treetops as well as the locust sounding like a chainsaw. I guess this is what it was like on the seventh day of creation.

—David Sifri
(fourth-grade descriptive essay)

CHAPTER 23

We Are One with Nature

The infinite beauty and sophistication in even the simplest plant or animal reminds us of the depth of life in our universe. As we connect with nature in this most spiritual way, we realize it is our Garden of Eden.

Walking across the sand, Karen feels the wind picking up, ominously announcing the onset of a storm. She feels the warm breeze begin to cool, and as if on cue, the ocean waves heighten. Soon the earthy smell of rain fills the air. Peering down, she notices the sand puckered with small indentations from the first raindrops. Moments later she finds herself in the midst of a downpour, enveloped by a deep sense of peace.

As daylight turns to dusk, flashes of lightning fill the sky. The crack of thunder is not far behind. Waves crash against the shoreline with increasing ferocity. The storm's energy radiates around and through her. Karen is filled with a sense of wonder and awe. The power and magnificence of nature is upon her.

$$\infty$$

The tree stood twelve to fifteen feet tall, its width equaling its height. The four trunks emerging from its base were covered with smooth whitish-gray bark strikingly accented with streaks of black. Its many spade-shaped leaves grew airily on widely spaced branches, allowing observers to enjoy a largely unobstructed view of the blue sky as the leaves moved freely in the wind.

It was a tree that loved to dance, and it would dance for anyone. One simply had to look at it to appreciate its beauty, to engage it in conversation. It stood alone, effortlessly emitting the light of God; its leaves, shimmering in the sun, fluttering like the wings of a multitude of butterflies.

I had first noticed the tree when I started going to the restaurant in the early morning hours to write. It stood outside in clear view of the patrons, the hostesses, the waitresses, and me. It sat on a downhill slope with its mid to upper parts most visible through the restaurant's front windows.

I had come to appreciate the interactive quality of plants and vegetation before my experience with the tree. I remember, while driving to Chicago some years earlier, that I had noticed a long, tall patch of frayed greenish-brown grass on the side of the highway. The grass was moving to and fro in the wind—swaying gently, rhythmically—singing to me of love and spirit. I began to understand that there was a level to nature other than the superficial one initially perceived, in which the grass simply moved with the surrounding air. On this higher level, there was so much more; God and life were in harmony, dancing in each other's arms, and I could feel it in my soul.

As I visited the restaurant daily, I couldn't help but notice a similar positive energy emanating from the tree. I started to feel an intimate connection with it. The hostess quickly picked up on my feelings and began to seat me at tables where I would have a clear view of the tree. After breakfast, I would often walk outside and gaze upon it.

In time, I noticed something unusual. When I focused my attention on the tree, it would begin to stir, even without the presence of the wind—as if awakening from a quiet slumber. Initially one or two branches would start to sway, causing the leaves to move delicately to and fro ... and then, suddenly, the entire tree would erupt with motion. It was dancing, slowly at first, with accented movements, and then at a quickened tempo, performing with the grace and beauty of a magnificently synchronized ballet, its leaves pirouetting like so many ballerinas—full of life and spirit. After a short period of time it would once again begin to settle, to rest.

I was reminded of the ever-present beauty of spirit. God would serenade me through every manifestation of his love if I chose to listen.

The energy of the world is unbelievable. One of its most beautiful char-
acteristics is it's always developing. It will never cease to learn because
that's the universe—it's all about growth.

Energy truly does flow through everything around you and of course
flows within you. Look at the detail of this earth, truly remarkable. Do
you know why that is? It's because you have helped to create it. Every
speck of sand has your energy in it. Every snowflake has a part of you
within it. Everything is one.

—David Sifri, a spiritual communication

CHAPTER 24

Does God Evolve?
Three Viewpoints

For many people with a traditional religious background, the concept of God evolving is unsettling. I would suggest, however, that *evolution is synonymous with growth*—with vibrancy and energy—with an ever-increasing state of beauty and purity.

For some, the difficulty arises from the concern that if God evolves, it must then follow that there is an element of instability in the spiritual universe. However, I feel differently. I find it exciting to think of God as such a dynamic being. With evolution, the spiritual possibilities seem endless and awe-inspiring.

I might equate God with a teacher. A great teacher never stops learning and experiencing; moreover, such teachers grow through their interactions with their pupils. Likewise, if we were to imagine

God as a parent, his experiences with his children would also be interactive. Just as parents are given the opportunity to teach their children, they are also given the opportunity to learn from them—to come to appreciate the wonder of life through their eyes.

I believe we are all contributing to the evolution of God because the experience of God is comprised, at least in part, of every one of our spiritual and life experiences. We are, after all, a part of God; we arose from him ... and will forever remain connected to him. He lives in us and through us.

Perhaps it is time for us to celebrate the opportunity to join with God in creating this ever-evolving, joyous spiritual adventure.

♋

Often people who believe that God does not evolve still conceive of God as a dynamic being. They are likely to view God as having a more separate identity than the one I portray. Hence, they feel their spiritual and life experiences do not directly affect God in a way that causes him to change. They find comfort in his consistency ... in the security that God is the same yesterday, today, and tomorrow.

The key is not so much whether we believe that God evolves but that discussions such as these, undertaken in a loving environment, help us each to further define our individual truths.

♋

I once asked a nun her thoughts on whether God evolves. She told me she did not believe that God evolves or changes. When I explained my reasoning—that our interactions with spirit and our personal growth experiences are likely to have some effect on God—she said she agreed that all of our life experiences affect God. But she went on to say that God is made up of all these experiences from the beginning to the end of time; God is every experience in every point in time that ever was or ever will be. From her standpoint, God does not evolve because God is already all of these experiences wrapped into one.

On reflection, I found her theory to be intriguing. She was saying that God transcends our limited concept of time; God simultaneously experiences the past, present, and future. He is simply every living experience.

CHAPTER 25

We Connect through Feelings

I asked a recent acquaintance of mine, Sonia, if she considered herself to be spiritual person. In response to the question, she said, "My grandfather is a minister, but I don't go to church often."

When I explained that I was asking more about spirituality than religion, Sonia still wasn't sure that she would describe herself as spiritual. She was uncertain as to whether she felt a connection with something greater.

Upon further reflection, however, Sonia recalled that she'd had a number of memorable church experiences. On every occasion, she had arrived at church feeling upset and on edge, but in each instance, the minister's sermon specifically addressed the difficulty with which she was struggling. On one Sunday, it was about whether to extend forgiveness to a friend who had hurt her deeply; on another, it was about taking advantage of the opportunity to extend love to a family member with whom she had become disgruntled. While Sonia listened to each sermon, she felt a serene peace come over her—a release of all tension as her heart filled with love.

During the course of each sermon, Sonia experienced an unusual sensation deep within, as if the minister were speaking directly to her ... as if *God* were communicating with her through this man of the cloth.

Several months after our discussion, I had another conversation with Sonia about spirituality. She had been doing some reading on the subject and had begun to feel more spiritually aware. By focusing her attention on whether her thoughts were arising from love or fear, she was becoming increasingly mindful of the influence her thoughts were having on creating her life experiences.

Sonia cited as an example a successful meeting she'd had recently with her employer's regional director. In the past, she would have worried about the meeting beforehand and focused on her perceived inadequacies, but prior to this meeting, she consciously envisioned that it would be positive. She believed this had created an atmosphere that virtually guaranteed good communication and success.

Sonia, who had been "super close" to her other grandfather while growing up, also spoke about her recent visits to his gravesite. Although she had always experienced a feeling of tranquility at the cemetery, she was becoming increasingly aware of her grandfather's loving presence as she shared her most intimate thoughts with him. Talking with him brought her a quiet, reassuring comfort. She knew he was listening.

Within the past year, Ashley had moved back to town, started a new job, and gotten married. I had last seen her when she was finishing college with plans to get an advanced degree in geriatric health care. At the time, I was impressed that someone so young felt drawn to helping the elderly. Ashley loved older people and wanted to work with them in a caring environment.

With her recent move and other life changes, Ashley was feeling stressed. I asked this soft-spoken newlywed if she considered herself to be spiritual. She answered that she did not feel a connection with any greater being or power, nor on an intellectual level did she believe that God existed.

I went on to ask Ashley if she had ever experienced a heightened sense of peace or love that might be interpreted as spiritual. Ashley told me that at times, when she performed acts of kindness for the nursing home residents, she would become tranquil. During these encounters, her mind would grow quiet; she was no longer distracted by life's everyday concerns.

Ashley's most memorable experiences came about through her close interactions with some of the nursing home residents who were in the process of dying. When these residents sensed it was their time to pass, they would become serene—almost transcendent. As Ashley reached out to them in a setting of quiet intimacy, she experienced utter peace.

To this day, Ashley still doubts the existence of God. Yet the blissful feeling she experienced with those dying patients—the heightened feeling of love and joy—remains a meaningful part of her life's journey.

Michelle, a close friend of mine whose carefree laugh speaks of her ever-present amusement with life, did her medical residency training at a university hospital. In her first year, she was frequently called on to handle emergencies or other difficult situations. If she could afford to wait five minutes before responding, she would retreat into a closet-sized room in the hospital. She considered it to be her sanctuary.

During this time, Michelle would sit with God. She would lean back in her chair, her feet stretched out lazily on the windowsill, and gaze outward. After a few minutes, she would pray for the strength and wisdom to handle the sick individuals who were depending on her. Upon leaving the room, Michelle always felt a sense of renewal. She basked in a feeling of peace and love—of oneness with the divine.

The other medical residents always commented on Michelle's uncanny serenity during stressful medical situations. Although they tried to emulate her approach when dealing with patients who were faltering, they were never able to radiate her aura of peace.

I will guide them.
I will turn darkness into light before them
And make the rough places smooth.

—Isaiah 42:16 NIV

CHAPTER 26

When We Feel Unease, It Is Time to Reconnect

Over time, we become better attuned to ourselves and more aware of when we feel less connected spiritually. We are less connected when we feel a diminished sense of joy or peace—when we feel a sense of emptiness or loneliness. These feelings of isolation may be accompanied by a sense of frustration or despair brought on by our tendency to dwell on the unpleasantness in our lives. When encountering such difficulties, it is helpful to quiet our minds and move once again toward the peace we have felt within. We reconnect through feelings—not thoughts. The mind only creates more anxiety.

It is natural for us to feel our connection with spiritual love ebb and flow. We are continually evolving spiritually, but at times we may feel that for every step forward, we are moving two steps backwards. During these times, we should try to reconnect through those methods that have worked well for us in the past. Prayer, meditation, music, writing, and humor are but a few of the mediums through which we can re-center ourselves.

❦

Darkness is not infinite
But love is

—Mitchell Kleinholz

Mitchell, the nine-year-old boy we first met in chapter 4, described his experience with an angel. It happened in church. At the front of the sanctuary were two sculptures of babies; each baby, arms outstretched toward a more central painting of God, was holding a book. In the painting, God had a long white beard and blue eyes. As Mitchell studied the painting, a "two-foot grayish clear ball" emerged from it and began zipping around the room. The ball sparkled and contained the vague image of a face. Mitchell could barely make out eyes and a mouth. The bottom of the ball was pointed "like a tail."

The ball started moving through the church aisles, searching for something. It eventually came to rest two feet in front of Mitchell and studied him intently, staring at him as if he were "some kind of freak or something." While Mitchell gazed at the ball, he found himself paralyzed.

After a short period of time, the ball began to move again and eventually settled at the front of the church. Just before reentering the painting, "it turned into a five-foot angel with golden wings—wings that were feathery, like the wings of an owl. The angel wore a white robe tied with a brown cloth. Its feet were bare."

That evening, Mitchell decided to return to the church. While his mother waited in the car, he knelt on the lawn, his head bowed in prayer. He had begun to wonder if the angel he had seen was real. As he communed with God, he felt a gust of wind. He looked up and saw the grass moving in waves, its motion whispering the gentle voice of spirit, its blades creating the impression of a twenty-foot cross. Mitchell interpreted the image as confirmation that he was on the right track, praying. Upon returning to the car, he noticed the cross had vanished.

Later that night as he lay in bed, Mitchell reflected on what he had seen. Was it real? Or had he simply imagined it all? He finally decided it didn't matter because, real or not, he was at peace. As Mitchell had quieted the outside noise, becoming one with the wind and the grass beneath him, he was reminded of the ever-present beauty of God, of the mysterious nature of spirit.

☙

In the winter of 1994, Sue's father died from lung cancer. Twelve years later, she shared her story with me in an e-mail and was kind enough to allow me to include it in this book:

> As my family and I were driving to my dad's graveside service, my mother asked to stop at a florist along the way. She wanted all four of us children to buy a flower to place atop our dad's casket.
>
> We went into the shop, where my mom picked out a long-stemmed red rose. I was reaching for my favorite, a long-stemmed peach-colored rose, when I heard my younger sister ask the florist if he had any sunflowers. I thought that a little unusual, snickered a bit, then was surprised to hear the florist say, sure, he had some in the back.
>
> As we headed back to the car, each of us clutching our single blossom, we laughed at Joan and her scraggly, unwieldy sunflower. I finally said, "What's the deal with the sunflower?" And Joan said, "You never saw Dad's sunflowers?"
>
> Apparently, during the years when I was in college, or abroad, I'd missed out on this family tale. It turned out that my dad, who had never been much

of a gardener, had decided one spring to plant some sunflower seeds in our Seattle-area backyard. It must have been an unusually sunny spring, because those plants grew to be eight feet tall or more, towering over my dad and the backyard fence. Joan remembered how much fun he'd had showing off those sunflower plants. Hearing the story, I knew I would never look at sunflowers the same way again.

A few weeks later, back home in Cincinnati, I was moping around, feeling sorry for myself, and decided to go to the mall. As I was driving across town, my dad was on my mind, and I recall thinking, *Dad, I wish there were some way to know that you're okay, that you got wherever you were going, and that it's okay there.*

I trudged aimlessly into the mall that spring day, wishing for some kind of sign that my dad was in a better place. Or that he was at least okay. But I didn't expect anything.

Out of habit, I headed toward Eddie Bauer, which when I was a kid had been a premier mountaineering outfitter and a favorite store to visit with my dad in old downtown Seattle. Nearby, I passed the Museum Store, which had in the display window a collection of artsy tote bags and such—each emblazoned with a large sunflower. Probably a Van Gogh theme. I thought of Joan's sunflower, smiled, and continued on.

A couple of stores later, I chuckled to myself as I saw a couple of manikins in the front window wearing T-shirts with sunflower images on the front. *Cute,* I thought, and started to feel a little better.

Then I headed toward the end of the mall. As I walked down the long walkway, I passed another display window and stopped in my tracks. There, completely filling the window, were sunflowers everywhere. In pots, on shirts, on tablecloths, on tote bags. The display was just overflowing with sunflowers and sunflower images.

This was *so much* something my dad would do, with his wry sense of humor, crooked smile, and quiet little chuckle. I started laughing, saying, "Okay, Dad, enough. I get it!"

I was still smiling as I walked into a large department store and felt his strong presence. Sure enough, as I headed into the kitchen store, there were still more sunflowers. On aprons, dish towels, tablecloths. I bought a couple of the dishtowels and headed out of the store. As I retraced my steps through the mall, I felt as if my dad and I were walking together, giving each other playful little shoves as we went.

I had entered that mall feeling terribly low and rather hopeless. And an hour or so later, I left laughing and feeling very hopeful. Somehow, I knew then that everything was okay. I still missed my dad greatly—particularly when I looked up at his favorite mountain, or wanted to share good news with him—but I stopped feeling *bad*.

A cynic might say that the spring of 1994 was simply the year of the great sunflower fad. Pure coincidence. Another year, it might be Beanie Babies. Or cute frogs. But I'm going to cling to the notion that it was more than that.

When I ask for help in the midst of overwhelming fear
That help is always forthcoming
Inviting me to quietly surrender ... to lovingly commune
With the infinite beauty and peace of God

CHAPTER 27

Spirituality and Prayer

*P*rayer is a fascinating subject. I am always intrigued by the different approaches people take to prayer—that is, how they personally connect with God. My son, when he was younger, told me he prayed by looking upward with his eyes wide open. He wanted to peer directly at God.

I remember listening to Elena, a medical resident, discuss how she approached prayer. We were having a round-table discussion about spirituality, and Elena was the last to speak. Her reluctance to talk about her spiritual experiences, and thereby draw attention to herself, served only to remind me of her humble nature.

Elena began her prayers in a state of appreciation. She expressed her gratitude to God as she would to a loving grandfather—one in whom she had absolute faith and from whom she had received much kindness. Elena would then enter a state of communion ... a place of increased receptivity. She was open to God's guidance and counsel, his wisdom and understanding, his love and warmth. She was with her most trusted companion, one who walked with her every moment of the day and upon whom she could always lean.

Listening to Elena, I felt God's overwhelming presence. Her communion with spirit left me in a state of awe. The energy was light and airy, as if one were awakening to a fresh dawn—the air cooled by the morning breeze, the sun peeking in with warmth.

The following story about spirit and faith is based on a young woman's Easter prayer. Like Christ's universal message of love and light, it transcends religion. And so I ask readers of *all faiths* to continue with the understanding that we are all woven of the same spiritual fabric—a fabric of peace and joy, of empowerment and beauty, of truth and unconditional love.

Jennifer, a close friend of mine, considered prayer to be "more like a conversation." She conversed with God throughout her day. Occasionally when Jennifer prayed, she felt distracted; during these times, it was difficult for her to feel spiritually connected. At other times, however, she was totally focused and found herself enveloped by feelings of love and security. During these instances, she would feel at peace. Her peace did not arise from a belief that her prayers were going to be answered but from a belief that someone was listening. Knowing that someone was listening brought Jennifer great comfort.

Jennifer did not believe in repeating a prayer request; asking once was enough. God was listening. One would have to trust that God would provide the best possible outcome. As she put it, "When you put your faith in someone else, it causes you not to worry. Your outlook changes."

It was Easter Sunday, and while Jennifer was in church, she decided to say a prayer. She had recently married and wanted a baby, but due to the fact that a number of her colleagues—three of whom were on fertility drugs—were finding it difficult to conceive, she was feeling apprehensive.

As Jennifer sat in church, she began her prayer with appreciation. She gave thanks for all the wonderful things in her life: her health, her husband, her family, her friends, her job, and her life. She was so grateful. While she conversed with God, Jennifer requested that she be able to bear children. She expressed the hope that she and her husband would become parents; she felt they had so much to offer a child. At the end of her prayer, Jennifer asked Jesus to come into her life, to help make her a better person, to guide her in the right direction. Upon finishing her prayer, Jennifer felt connected; she knew God was listening.

Within a couple of weeks, Jennifer began to feel physically and emotionally different; something was going on inside of her, "something weird." It was hard for her to describe exactly how she felt, except to note that she was a little more tired than usual. The pregnancy test that Jennifer took before the recommended waiting period confirmed what she already knew. She was with child.

Three months later, Jennifer excitedly informed me of her condition. We were meeting to have dinner with her husband and her sister, spirituality being the evening's topic of discussion. Although I found the ensuing conversation intriguing, especially when her husband spoke of the unconditional love and acceptance he believed everyone would experience at the end of their lives, I could tell Jennifer was distracted. She seemed uncharacteristically disengaged from what was being shared.

The following day as I thought about our dinner, I intuitively felt that something was going on with Jennifer. I called and told her that I sensed she was seeking a greater understanding of something spiritual and powerful, something life-changing but not yet identifiable. She said that she didn't know of what spiritual matter I might be speaking.

The next day, I received a phone call from Jennifer. She proceeded to tell me how she had completely forgotten about her prayer experience until our conversation the day before. On reflection, Jennifer couldn't help but wonder if the prayer incident was the spiritual experience of which I spoke—about how she had prayed that she be able to have children and then became pregnant one and a half weeks later, despite the fact that she was thirty-one years old and had recently been on birth-control pills. The evening before she called me, she had related the Easter prayer to her husband. She told me of her husband's surprise that she had never shared her meaningful experience with him—the feeling of certainty that someone was listening as she expressed her desire to have a child. In the excitement of her pregnancy, amid the joyful noise of motherhood, she had forgotten her Easter prayer, even though she had continued to converse with God on a daily basis.

The next time we met, I asked Jennifer how the prayer experience had affected her. With a smile on her face and a humbled look of astonishment, she excitedly told me she felt empowered. She went on to say, "I can ask for things, pray for things, and things will happen! Somebody is paying attention!"

Yet I knew from our conversations that what Jennifer cherished most was her close relationship with God—the feeling that someone indeed was listening. This was, in part, the reason she had forgotten about her Easter prayer. When Jennifer prayed, she was focused on the present moment. She was expressing her inner desires and appreciating the warmth with which her requests were being received. She was not looking ahead but within—immersed in a state of bliss.

ॐ

How do we reconcile Jennifer's story with the couple who is praying for their sick child or the woman who has been trying unsuccessfully to become pregnant for years? Is it possible that all prayers are answered, perhaps just not in the manner that we might imagine? Consider this scenario:

> As a sick child lies in bed, her loving father prays
> beside her. His prayer begins with thanks. He offers

appreciation for his wonderful family, his sweet daughter, his ability to provide. During his prayer, he begins to feel the peaceful and unending love of spirit. His mind becomes still—tears roll down his face. In the midst of worry and darkness, he finds beauty, reassurance, and light.

In this setting, we are better able to understand the essence of prayer, to understand that every step along a prayer path is meaningful. We recognize that our most wonderful prayer experiences come through trust and a loving state of mind.

☙

Antonio, a first-generation Italian American, was brought up in a traditional Catholic church. The God of his youth was stern, judgmental, and distant—one at whom he would violently shake his fist while giving the one-finger salute.

Over time, however, Antonio's perception of God changed. The God of his childhood was no longer the one of his present world. His new God was gentle and loving, focused on helping Antonio tap into the wonders of the universe.

Antonio was divorced with two grown children. He was a good father and provider, but he didn't feel fulfilled. Recent life changes had caused him to reassess the course he'd chosen as well as his future path. Although he had tried to combine his passion for creativity with his occupation of creating and duplicating art, it was unsatisfying. He also yearned for a meaningful personal relationship, someone with whom he could share his most intimate thoughts and feelings.

Antonio's real passion was writing. He wanted to write a novel about a modern-day Christ, an individual who at first might not be recognized but who would eventually come to remind others of the beauty of spirit: a person who would perform good works and miracles and, more importantly, radiate love—the pure spirit of God.

Antonio's greatest challenge was finding a balance between his reality and fulfilling his passion. He feared that if he allowed himself to become totally absorbed in his spiritual writings, he would cease to live in the real world. He would write day and night with total abandon. Because of this concern, Antonio chose to proceed cautiously. He would keep both feet anchored on the ground and merely dabble in the world of the unseen.

When Antonio's abilities were exhausted and he needed the light of inspiration to show him the way, he would immediately go to prayer ... like a Muslim responding to the call from the mosque. Kneeling at his bedside, hands covering his eyes, he would commune with God. Antonio did not engage in prayer halfheartedly. It required his undivided attention, and he would undertake it with an open heart and a focused mind. He would communicate with God as lovers do after intimate relations—"in the afterglow"—facing each other without reservation or hesitancy, in open and loving honesty.

Antonio started his prayer by acknowledging that God's form is expressed in everything, his beauty apparent in all of life. He felt "privileged to be alive ... here to witness God's creation ... to grow internally." Antonio believed the sum of all our life experiences lead us to "complete awareness," as we spiritually grow through multiple lifetimes.

"We are God rediscovering himself!" Antonio proclaimed with an intensity that carried an almost electrical charge, as if lightning and thunder were advancing to trumpet this wonderful truth, to unveil this powerful mystery.

Every prayer request of Antonio's varied. On one day, his appeal to God might be as follows: "Enable me to see that you are a part of everything. Instead of my focus being on the mundane, allow me to see your hand in every aspect of my life, to be amazed by every aspect of my life, so that I may be filled with love." On another day, he might simply ask God for help, to assist him in becoming one with spirit and purpose.

After expressing his request, Antonio would visualize his prayer moving outward. He would project this imagery wholeheartedly, picturing his thought radiating from the rotating earth in a golden fan-like distribution, out to the solar system, and then to the universe at large. Eventually he would envision his prayer traveling a great distance from Earth—light-years away—still intact and powerful, defining his life and his truth.

Antonio continued to feel connected and peaceful after prayer. He was left in a state of reverent communion knowing that his prayer had been received.

The manifestations of Antonio's prayer were always immediate and astonishing. God would speak in the mystical language of beauty and love, leaving Antonio feeling joyful, appreciative, and empowered.

Despite his remarkable prayer experiences, Antonio chose to pray only occasionally. He feared that if he drew any closer to the spiritual realm, he might never return to the world of human existence. His trust would establish the limits of his spiritual experience ... the breadth of his opportunity to revel in the beauty of God.

A hand of love
Is extended with seeds of hope
And then through faith
A miracle is born

Jeremy was born early, at twenty-four weeks, weighing one pound, thirteen ounces. He was baptized on the night of his birth. His Catholic parents named him after the prophet Jeremiah. Given his premature delivery and low birth weight, they felt he needed a strong name. They were right.

For weeks following Jeremy's birth, it was touch and go. Jeremy's parents, Kim and Charles, practically lived at the hospital. When Jeremy was one month old, Kim received a phone call from the hospital telling her that her son's heart rate was very low—fifteen beats per minute. Could she come up with her husband to say their final good-byes?

It was 2:00 a.m. when Kim and Charles arrived at the hospital. They were reluctant to enter the building, afraid of what they might encounter. Instead, they sat in the parking lot talking, crying, and praying. Before going in, Kim had a candid conversation with God. "God, if you're going to take him, please take him now. He can't go through any more, and we can't go through any more. If he is going to make it, please give us a sign." She was young and desperate, twenty-three and grasping.

Afterwards, as Kim held her son in the neonatal intensive-care unit, she noticed a man standing near her. Dressed in surgical scrubs, he had short brown hair and nondescript features. As his eyes focused on hers, she found herself being drawn in. His "soulful eyes" were intense yet comforting.

"It is through Jesus that God hears," the man said while gazing at her.

Moments later, Kim looked down at her son and began to pray. She asked Jesus to please ask God to heal her son. Her prayer, however, was different from what it had been earlier. Before, she was just saying the words. Now it was "from the heart—not just an empty plea but a conversation—a lifeline." After repeating the prayer several times, her son's heart rate began to rise steadily. It continued to rise until it eventually normalized.

When Kim looked around for the man in the scrubs, he was nowhere to be found. She asked the nurses on the unit who he was. They said there had been no man in the unit other than her husband. There had been no other parents, no other male nurses, no other male doctors. Although Charles had also seen him, the man simply didn't exist as far as the nurses were concerned.

The next day, Kim's son was moved into another hospital room reserved for very sick children. One of the medical residents told Kim, nonchalantly, that she might want to consider disconnecting her son from the machines. He is "going to be a vegetable anyway," he said.

Kim responded by declaring, "Then he is going to be my vegetable, and I will take care of him!"

Jeremy is now twenty-three years old. He is blind, has cerebral palsy with left-sided weakness, and a keen intellect. Another one of Kim's sons, Kevin, also has cerebral palsy and is confined to a wheelchair. Her third son is free of any serious health issues. Kim is truly appreciative for the gift of her children; she sees so much beauty in each of her sons.

People occasionally look at Kim with pity and ask her, "How do you do it?" And she thinks, *I don't know any different; it's not like a punishment.* Rather, she feels truly blessed.

When Jeremy was in high school, one of his essays caught Kim's attention. In the essay, Jeremy wrote of his desire to see, as well as of his acceptance of his blindness. Kim was reminded of the hospital resident who had suggested that she turn off Jeremy's life-support equipment when he was an infant. For years, she had carried a profound sense of guilt resulting from her children's maladies. It was her own medical condition that had led to their early deliveries, resulting in one child's inability to see and another child's inability to walk. And so, she decided to ask Jeremy if she had made the right choice, if she had been wise in not following the resident's advice. As she told Jeremy the story, he couldn't believe that the resident had suggested shutting off his life-support equipment.

"He really asked you that, Mom?" he said, adding, "I'm glad you didn't!"

Hearing this answer brought Kim a newfound peace.

As Kim reflects on her hospital experience, she feels certain the man in the surgical scrubs was an angel. With quiet appreciation, she expressed to me her gratitude for having been able to experience such a precious gift.

I asked Kim why she needed to pray to God through Jesus. What was the significance? She told me that Jesus made her prayer more personal. He had experienced life as a human; he understood struggles and emotions. She could identify with him.

Previously she had simply been going through the motions with prayer, but now Kim knew *there was something else out there.*

❧

Caroline, a seventy-year-old patient, asked me during an office visit whether I believed in God. After I responded in the affirmative, she asked me if I believed in miracles. With my interest piqued, I told her I did. She then proceeded to tell me a story.

Caroline and her husband had lived in the same house for a long period of time. For reasons she didn't disclose to me, over the past thirty-four years they hadn't spoken a word to each other. Her husband, Rudi, kept everything that was needed for his daily living in the basement and seldom spent much time upstairs. When Caroline would return home, Rudi would scurry like an animal into another room or go downstairs.

Six months before she came to see me, Caroline had begun praying that God would touch Rudi's heart. Caroline and Rudi both had health problems, and, considering their advancing ages, Caroline felt they needed each other. She prayed that Rudi would forgive her so they could once again become friends. After years of living separate lives, she wasn't expecting that they would behave like husband and wife, but she was hoping they could at least communicate and live together in peace.

Two months before her visit, Caroline's routine blood work revealed that she had leukemia. She didn't tell any of her family members. She did, however, begin praying more. She was afraid, and she felt very alone. Caroline had felt so full of life, but now she felt her life was coming to an end. She appealed to God for courage and strength.

As she knelt in prayer, she proclaimed, "I am going to need this man!"

She asked God to send the Holy Spirit to Rudi's heart, knowing it would be hard for Rudi to make peace. His pride ran deep.

Two weeks later, Rudi came up behind her.

"Caroline?" he said, with a tenderness she hadn't heard in years.

"Yes?" she answered as she turned slowly.

"I've been thinking," he continued somewhat hesitantly. "You've been a very good mother to the children. I left you when you needed me the most, when you were raising the kids. I wonder if you can find it in your heart to forgive me?"

Caroline steadied herself.

With tears streaming down her cheeks, she responded, "Yes. You know I don't hold grudges. I forgive you."

As Caroline spoke the words, she felt herself being lifted supernaturally.

Later, when she returned to her bedroom, she exclaimed, "Lord, you are so fast!"

PART VI

Find and Express Your Truths

Each of us is a God
Each of us knows all
We need only open our minds
To hear our own wisdom

—Buddha

CHAPTER 28

Life Gives Us the Opportunity to Express Who We Are

John is a physician who shines in academic settings. He is a voracious reader whose mind contains a wealth of information. He is the doctor who graduated at the top of his medical class, who was taught to follow his intellect over his feelings. He is also the doctor whose wife developed breast cancer at an early age and literally experienced the light of God one night as she lay deathly ill in the hospital while undergoing chemotherapy. She is the determined woman who went on to defy the odds and have two more children after chemo-induced menopause.

A few years after his wife's recovery, John went on a spiritual retreat with some fellow church members. During that weekend, he and the other parishioners shared their life stories with one another.

At one point during the retreat, John sat on his bed reading letters of affection from those close to him. As he felt the love of family and friends wash over him, he found himself opening his heart to God.

After reading his children's letters and looking at their colorful artwork, John dropped to his knees. Their simple expressions of love without reservation touched him on the deepest of levels, causing him to realize that he was going through the motions of life without truly experiencing the joy of living.

For years John had experienced little peace. His medical practice was demanding, and he frequently found himself preoccupied with concerns of financial security. He enjoyed spending time with his four young children, but their noisy behavior often provided an additional stress, causing him to feel the need to escape.

As John came to better understand what it was that he was seeking—a feeling of wellness within—he decided it was time to let go. Amid unstoppable tears, he sincerely and humbly asked God for joy. He asked not for a superficial joy but a deep joy, a feeling of rightness within.

John was answered with an overwhelming sense of peace, a release of all his anxieties. His everyday worries melted away. There was no more conflict between his wants and his needs, only a feeling of wholeness and simplicity. He didn't need to obtain more things. He needed only love and clarity of purpose, the company of family and friends.

I remember seeing John shortly after his experience. As he entered the spacious room, I couldn't help but take notice. His spiritual energy was breathtaking ... of biblical proportions. It preceded him, enveloped him. It was a comforting energy—warm, light, rich. It filled empty spaces.

John was detached but present, his being no longer tethered to earth. His focus was in the moment ... his mind quiet, his heart open. He was ever aware of the beauty of life, the blessings bestowed on all of us. Immersed in the ebb and flow of spirit, he was gliding through life on a higher plane, a plane undisturbed by the everyday challenges of human existence. He had experienced the light within, and now he was radiating it silently, gently. He was in this world but not of it, joyfully immersed in love.

Since his experience, John feels a renewed love for his wife and children. He understands that to continue to be at peace spiritually, he must work at it, feed it, still his mind, and reconnect. When John invests in prayer and other spiritual endeavors, he once again visits the mountaintop, once again catches a glimpse of heaven.

A year after his retreat, I received a card from John in which he expressed his appreciation of our friendship and of my efforts to write about my spiritual truths. What struck me most about his card was the warmth he expressed and the ease with which he spoke from his heart. The closing, *"Love, John,"* was un-self-consciously penned in his childlike handwriting. I was deeply touched by his caring words and realized how much John has continued to grow since his experience with the light within. That weekend he asked God for joy in a setting of surrender, and his faith delivered it.

When Ron was in seminary, he thought his Catholic religion was the True Faith. He reveled in the laws of the church—laws that were black and white and that made it easy to differentiate right from wrong. Eventually, though, he came to believe that religion was not about laws but about people—people whose actions were not black and white but shades of gray. He also came to believe that God was bigger than any one faith. "Why would God say *we* are the best, and that's it?" he asked.

He added that every religion has different strengths from which we all can learn. The Jewish faith, for instance, has its rich traditions, emphasizing cleanliness, the law, the sacred word. Theirs is a God of justice as well as one of love. Muslims, likewise, have a God of righteousness. They worship daily, with reverence—with piousness. And in the Protestant churches, the Baptists preach with fire; they speak from the heart.

Ron went on to say the Catholic Mass, on the other hand, is planned out from beginning to end, spontaneity and passion often lacking. "People go to church to be lifted up," he stated. "As the parishioners plod through their workweek, coping with the daily grind, they're looking to be recharged on Sundays, looking for something beyond the ephemeral." When Ron watched them in church, he realized that the experience was potentially numbing; it was all so theoretical.

Since the fifth grade, Ron had known he wanted to be a priest. As a teenager, he treasured his high school seminary experience. There was such a sense of community. He remembers going to city parks and caring for the gardens. He recollects the feeling of brotherhood between the priests and students—the honest, hard work that took place in the impoverished areas of Detroit.

When Ron advanced to his college seminary, however, things were quite different. Priests there were pompous and disengaged from the students. Many of them drank heavily and seemed more concerned with advancing their own careers than helping the downtrodden. Their greatest ambition appeared to be achieving a high enough status to qualify for their own MasterCard. The campus had a bowling alley, a swimming pool, and a gym second to none, but it offered no sense of community.

Ron struggled during his first year there. "What the hell is going on?" he wondered. He chafed at the disconnect he noticed between the beautiful rooms in the college and the struggling surrounding community.

Eventually he confronted the head of the seminary.

"This place is out of control!" Ron declared. "The priests seem less interested in serving God and ministering to parishioners than they are in living the good life themselves! When do you plan on changing things?" he demanded.

With his anger rising, he added, "I'm telling you, things are going to change!"

The provost rose out of his chair, yelling back at him, letting him know his criticism was not welcome. Eventually things did change, and a number of priests were shipped out, but unfortunately for Ron, it was too late. During his second year, he left the seminary, his dream washed away.

Ron still has some wonderful memories from his time in the seminary, however—heartening experiences that arose from individual efforts by fellow students to help the surrounding community. He remembers going to blighted neighborhoods where he and his classmates would fix the plumbing and perform other services for needy residents. At one home, he was met by a woman and her two young children. The house was in complete disrepair. The vanity was pulling away from the wall, and a number of the windows were broken, but it didn't take long for Ron to come to understand that this woman was more interested in having someone to talk to than in having her residence repaired. Just being able to converse with someone would be the highlight of her day—before her volatile husband returned home to raise hell. As Ron and his friend sat down with her, she offered them cake and coffee. Ron later discovered that her refrigerator was empty; she had offered them the only food in the house. He left feeling humbled.

On another occasion, Ron, who was multilingual, went to visit an elderly German woman who was dying in the hospital. Anna was in her eighties with no living relatives. She didn't interact with the nurses and was barely responsive. Since Ron spoke German, the nurses had asked him if he would come and spend some time with her.

As Ron began talking to Anna, he asked her how she was feeling. "I'm ready to go home," she said. "Where is everyone else?" she went on to ask.

Ron answered, "They've already passed on." After pausing for a moment, he added, "Anna, it's okay. Everything is done here."

An hour later, Anna died.

Ron also remembers a rabbi asking him to visit one of the Jewish patients in the hospital, one whom he thought didn't needed to be there but who was now scheduled for surgery. The rabbi said, "I've got a patient here, a hypochondriac. Would you mind stopping in and seeing her?"

"I figure if I send in a Catholic, it will scare her," the rabbi added with a smile.

As Ron entered the room, Ella asked, "What are you here for?" When Ron explained that the rabbi had asked him to stop by to see her, she replied, "What did he do that for?" Ron started to tell her that the rabbi was concerned about her, but before he could finish, Ella began talking about all of her medical problems. The complaints were never-ending. When Ron moved in nearer to get a better look at her, he could see no signs of the multiple ailments of which she complained. In fact, she appeared quite healthy.

After some time, Ron asked Ella if she understood that she was going to have an operation the next day based on her complaints. He looked directly into her eyes and tried to make sure that she grasped the connection between her perceived maladies and the impending surgery. Shortly thereafter, he left.

A few days later, Ron ran into the rabbi. "What did you say to Ella?" the rabbi asked him with a smile. "She had a miraculous recovery after your visit," he added, "and was discharged from the hospital the next day."

After Ron finished telling me these stories, I asked him what he had learned from his time in the seminary.

"I no longer have a desire to be intimately involved with the parishes but more of a desire to help people," he said. "Instead of praying at Mass, we need to focus on helping each other. This is something that cannot be institutionalized."

Ron went on to say that at the end of the day, we will all evaluate our lives based on the "smallest act of charity done for another, not on how often we go to church. People can go to church every Sunday because they like to, but that's not what it's about."

It isn't that Ron doesn't enjoy a beautiful Latin Mass, for he has a deep love of the Catholic Church. Rather, he sees an opportunity to make the religious experience richer, understanding that there are many paths to God. Ron recognizes that we can learn from one another, that every religion has something unique and meaningful to offer. Yet religion is only the starting point. Most important is the love we show each other—those little acts of kindness. That is where the beauty of God resides.

What is creation
If it's not joy
And liveliness of spirit

—Lou Kroner

CHAPTER 29

Live Your Passion

*W*hat is my passion?
This is one of the most important questions we can ask ourselves. Our passion is strongly connected with our being. It is our spirituality shining through.

It brings out the best in us, allowing us to sense our infinite potential.

❦

Lou, who taught both of my children, is a remarkable teacher. His easy smile, soft, reassuring voice, and comforting and attentive eyes all reflect his gentle nature.

Whenever Lou meets a new student, he looks at that child as he might a rare flower. Whether that flower is a shy eight-year-old girl or an energetic twelve-year-old boy, there is much to appreciate. As Lou focuses his love and attention on these children, they grow and blossom.

It is difficult not to feel Lou's passion during school activities. The atmosphere at such events is always positively charged. At a class poetry reading, I was amazed to see such peaceful elementary students. It wasn't that the kids were necessarily quiet or still but that they were relaxed and happy. After they finished reading their poetry, Lou stood and read his own. He was no different from them.

As a gifted educator, Lou inspires these students—these flowers—by sensing their enormous potential and cultivating it, by nurturing the soil to enrich their roots. And as these exquisite plants bloom, Lou's imprint is unmistakable—the product of care given in a setting of love, light, and excellence.

One day, I was walking our two dogs at a nearby park with my children when we came upon a stray. It was an Australian shepherd, a cross between a German shepherd and Alaskan husky, and was whining for attention. Unable to find a ranger, we left the dog in the care of some other people and returned home.

When my wife, Raye Ann, who is passionate about the welfare of children and animals, heard this, she decided to go back to the park to check on the dog. Since the people at the park couldn't provide long-term care, she brought it home—though she wasn't sure what we would do with a third dog. She posted notices in the neighborhood and on the Internet to no avail. By the next day, this large dog was dominating our smaller ones, and we knew that keeping him in our home was not a viable solution. Raye Ann took the dog to an animal shelter where she was assured it would be well taken care of and would be put up for adoption if not claimed. She continued to worry about the dog, though, checking on it regularly and continuing to post ads.

At one point, we received a call from a person named Emily who wanted another dog. Emily didn't have transportation, so Raye Ann offered to take her to the shelter to help her adopt it. Emily rejected my wife's offer. Even after Raye Ann explained to Emily that she herself would have to fill out the adoption papers, she still wanted Raye Ann to bring the dog to her. It soon became apparent that Emily wasn't willing to assume the responsibility of caring for the dog, and eventually she stopped calling. Raye Ann, however, continued to feel responsible for the dog. If no one adopted it, she planned to move the dog to a private no-kill shelter that, for a fee to cover costs, would actively look for a new owner.

I am happy to report that within two weeks the Australian shepherd found a new home.

I am funny and athletic
I am curious about the world
I am the popcorn popping in the microwave
I am the sun at the end of the day
I desire that no one is hungry, hurt, or
unhappy as long as I shall live
I am funny and athletic

I pretend there is no violence or war
I am the touch of fire after being in the cold
What bothers me is when people are not nice
When I see others hurt, it makes me sad
I am funny and athletic

I know that love is true
I believe in God above
I dream to be a princess in a perfect world
I try to get good grades and help others like
He does above
I desire to get an education and to have a
family full of love
I am funny and athletic

—Suzanne Sifri (eighth-grade school poem)

CHAPTER 30

Tell the Universe Your Truths

If we are created in the image and likeness of God, then, like him, we possess immeasurable creative powers; however, we may not fully realize the power that lies within our thoughts, words, and actions.

In order to comprehend the scope of our God-given creative abilities, we need to explore and purposefully utilize these gifts. Like God, we need to create rather than to react. Instead of trying to understand the truths of the universe, we need to tell the universe our truths. For this to occur, we must first quiet our minds. We can't tell the universe our truths before we know what our truths are, and we can't know what our truths are until we go within.

What are your truths? When my son used to go to his tae kwon do tests, his master instructor had the students stand and shout "I am" statements, such as "I am great!" He understood the power within such statements.

By making these declarations, we are telling the universe our truths … we are creating.

In the past, I have thought and said such declarations aloud. Depending on my focus at the time, I might say, "I am love, I am peace, I am joy!" These statements are empowering. They are also another way of connecting. On the other hand, declarations such as "I am tired," "I am miserable," or "Why is this happening to me?" are manifestations of low energy and are limiting.

When we feel a sense of disunity, the following declarations can be strong connectors: "I am one with spiritual love," or "I feel God's presence in everything I do." One of my favorites is "I am the light."

A more mystical declaration that is frequently recited during meditations is the phrase "I am." It is a powerful statement that serves to quiet the mind while reaffirming our limitless nature and our eternal union with the divine.

Another way we may choose to create is by envisioning our life as we intend it to be. As we think and talk about our life unfolding in a certain manner, we send our truths out into the universe. This is akin to an athlete mentally picturing the running of a race or the skiing of a slalom course before the beginning of a competition. Knowing the opportunity is being created as we think about it and offering

gratitude for it in advance is important—as is fully immersing ourselves in the experience.

Yet while we have a great ability to create our experiences through
visualization, we must remember that if for some reason these visu-
alizations do not fully blossom, it is likely because a higher spiritual
opportunity is awaiting us. In other words, it is important for us to
not be tied to the outcome. We are creating in this moment, or in a
series of moments, *and then letting go*—trusting in the universe. It is
also helpful for us to remember that the timing of such events is often
unpredictable. Life remains full of surprises.

As I have come to think about and express my feelings with this
book, I have done so with the growing knowledge that it has become
a powerful tool in creating my truths:

> I have told many people I am writing a book on spir-
> ituality and that I believe it will be meaningful. I
> have given thanks for the experience, knowing *in this
> moment* that the book will be published and that it
> will touch many. I have embraced the feelings of joy,
> peace, and love that have arisen through the writing,
> and I have celebrated the spiritual exchanges that have
> occurred as I have shared preliminary copies with
> friends and acquaintances.

All of this has served to enrich my experience, but if for some
reason the publishing of this book is significantly delayed, or if it
does not occur at all, I trust that a greater spiritual opportunity awaits
me—that the universe will unfold as it should. My greatest joy comes
not from anticipating the future gifts this book may bring but from
relishing each moment I have experienced in its creation.

I believe the most powerful and meaningful way to create is through
energy—connecting with our love within and inviting the most wonderful experiences unto ourselves. In this setting we are not creating

through thought but through being. We are experiencing the highest state of love and light and attracting similar types of energy unto us. We are living life to the fullest—in the present moment—and allowing the universe to respond in kind. In such a setting, we come to view every experience through the eyes of the soul—through loving eyes that see, feel, and appreciate everything with innocence and wonder.

Over time, I have come to embrace this type of creating. Rather than envisioning a specific future for myself, I engage in activities that quiet my mind and allow me to feel the love of spirit. In these circumstances, I am creating through my union with God. I am trusting in the universe—in the divine energy that flourishes in a setting of stillness and peace—as I fully surrender.

We are continually stating our truths to the universe whether we are aware of it or not. So the question each of us needs to consider is ...

"Do I want to create intentionally and with clarity of purpose?"

State your truths every day with the most wonderful thoughts and feelings. Send appreciation to God and yourself for bringing forth the most uplifting spiritual experiences. Allow the heightened energy of love and light to engulf you.

Seize the day!

☙

I was told by one of my patients to watch people as they sing in church. She spoke of the energy, the height of appreciation, and the willingness of the parishioners to sing their truths with abandon.

Gather together in one the children of God.

—*John 11:52 KJV*

Occasionally I recall a distant memory that brings me much joy. I remember being in the third grade on the day before Thanksgiving, standing on a platform and singing some songs. I was eight years old at the time and attending a non-parochial, private school. In keeping with the season, the walls of the large room were adorned with images of bountiful harvests—corn, pumpkins, wheat, and other gifts from the earth. Splashed about the room was the colorful plumage of handcrafted paper turkeys, simple creations that spoke of our youthful innocence.

The mood was one of celebration—of appreciation. This was a time of peace, friendship, family, and thanksgiving.

As I stood on that platform singing in the company of my classmates, I looked out into the audience where my mother was listening. There were a few rows of chairs, but others were scattered randomly around the room, giving the event a certain informality, a casualness that allowed people to move about freely and visit with one another. It was a festive atmosphere. A number of tables were overflowing with delicious food and drinks: hot chocolate, cinnamon-spiced apple cider, fresh baked goods, and sweets.

The aura of peace that washed over me that day was astounding. It was a warm sensation of joy and brotherhood that I would remember throughout my adult years. I don't recall any specific interactions that day with my mother, my friends, or my siblings. I just remember feeling that wonderful sensation of love, oneness, and happiness.

I connected with something greater that day, but I was unable to identify what in particular had brought me such heightened joy. About forty years later, clarity came. While walking through a grocery store around Thanksgiving, I heard the song "We Gather Together," and then, as those warm childhood memories washed over me anew, it hit me.

At the time, I was shopping for a gathering not unlike that school program forty years earlier. It would be a time of celebration, love, and giving thanks, as my family, including an out-of-town sister, gathered in a relaxed setting to break bread. People could move about freely on this occasion, too, enjoying each other's fellowship. As I recognized the similarities between the two gatherings, I came to understand that it had been the singing of this song, in the company of friends and family—in a setting of love and spirit—that had moved me so deeply forty years earlier.

Why it took me so long to equate the feeling I had while listening to the singing of "We Gather Together" with the same feeling of joy I experienced at my third-grade Thanksgiving program, I will never know. Yet I am not surprised that the experience had such a profound effect on me, because it is such a powerful song. It is an ode to brotherhood, praise, and thanks—one that speaks to our higher nature—to the beauty of our oneness with God. It serves to remind us that God is with us forever—that love is what unites us—and that it is through appreciation that we rise to our highest state.

> *We gather together to ask the Lord's blessing;*
> *He chastens and hastens His will to make known.*
> *The wicked oppressing now cease from distressing.*
> *Sing praises to His Name; He forgets not His own.*
>
> *Beside us to guide us, our God with us joining,*
> *Ordaining, maintaining His kingdom divine;*
> *So from the beginning the fight we were winning;*
> *Thou, Lord, were at our side, all glory be Thine!*
>
> *We all do extol Thee, Thou Leader triumphant,*
> *And pray that Thou still our Defender will be.*
> *Let Thy congregation escape tribulation;*
> *Thy Name be ever praised! O Lord, make us free*

—translated by Theodore Baker

For it is in giving, that we receive ...
And it is in dying that we are born to eternal life

—*Saint Francis of Assisi*

CHAPTER 31

Give What You Would
Like to Receive

Give what you would like to receive. This may sound counter-
intuitive, but when we want something, we are sending out
to the universe the message that says "I *want* something" or "I *need*
something." If we understand that we have the power to create—that
everything we think, say, and do has an effect—we begin to realize
the power of our thoughts, words, and actions. We begin to use empowering phrases like *I am* or *I intend to create.*

Likewise, if we *give* what we *want*, we are creating in the most
joyful manner. In giving, we are telling the universe this is a part of
who we are. For instance, if we desire compassion, we give compassion
to others. By doing so, we are boldly stating to the universe and to
ourselves that we *are* compassion.

During my years in practice, the wonderful staff in my office was
made up of many caring individuals, but even the most dedicated
among them often found it challenging to deal with difficult patients.
Our receptionist, Sue, however, was always able to see situations from
the patient's point of view. One could feel her empathy simply by listening to her answer the telephone. Her gentle voice comforted and
soothed even the most apprehensive patients.

Sue appeared genuinely happy to see each patient as they entered the office. Like a mother greeting her children after school, she was warm and welcoming. Her biggest frustration was when paperwork kept her from spending more time visiting with the patients. At the same time, these patients energized her by returning her kindness with love and appreciation. I believe the healing process for many of our patients began through first encountering her beautiful spirit.

As we give of ourselves, we reconnect in a most meaningful way. When we give with charity in our hearts, we are left with a wonderful feeling of fulfillment. The most powerful gift we can give is our love, so the next time you need love, give love. At this point, you are reminding yourself, and the universe, that you *are* love.

My daughter's select basketball coach, Mike, was just such a person. He gave of himself completely. During the team's extensive travels, he was always there for the girls. When they were experiencing some type of emotional crisis, they often found it easier to talk to Mike than their own parents.

As the girls shared their concerns about their mothers and fathers with Mike, he would get a sheepish look on his face and with the hint of a smile, say, "You know, as parents, we really don't know what we're doing."

The girls would laugh, but Mike's humor incorporated an underlying truth; it was just as scary being a parent as it was a teenager.

Mike was financially generous to a fault, yet he seemed uncomfortable if any appreciation was offered for his generosity. One Christmas he gave each of the girls a gift certificate for a mother-daughter spa treatment. To these fourteen-year-old girls, it was like giving them the world. They were beaming—dreaming of how they would indulge themselves.

There was nothing practical about the gift; it was simply a gift from the heart ... a gift of love because such was Mike's nature.

❦

Dean is a psychologist who told me during an office visit that he was thinking of changing his focus to writing children's books in the belief that he could create healing stories for them using the concepts of love and empowerment. Upon hearing his reasons for a contemplated career change, I steered the conversation toward his ideas on spirituality in general.

While we talked, Dean shared his thoughts with me about charitable contributions. He had found that no matter how much he donated, even if the gift were a financial stretch, he always got back more than he gave.

As Dean's eyes met mine, an inviting and playful smile appeared on his face. Having discovered something remarkable, he wished to share it with me.

"You can't out-give God!"

❦

When I think of my father, I still feel his warmth, kindness and unconditional love—reminiscent of the love of Christ. I never met a more selfless man, but his nature simply reflected the fact that he derived his greatest pleasure from helping others. I remember how he prepared for hours, every week, before meeting my ten-year-old son, David, on Fridays for science experiments that were not required for his schooling but were undertaken to further my son's understanding of physics, biology, and chemistry. In the process, my father was able to share his passion for knowledge with his grandson.

One of my father's favorite experiments was to place a piece of paper over a completely full glass of water, forming a seal between the paper, water, and rim of the glass. He would then show how the paper kept the water in place when the glass was turned over, demonstrating the effect of a vacuum. Although my father had undertaken this experiment countless times with his other grandchildren, he seemed just as fascinated doing the experiment with David as he had been the first time he performed it. Such was his approach to the world, one of curiosity and wonderment.

I also recall my father's inexhaustible patience in filling out extensive insurance forms to help my brother, Mike, establish his medical practice. Mike was in Washington, DC, finishing his residency, while my father was eagerly awaiting his return to Cincinnati. Day after day, I found my father sitting at the living room table methodically plowing through insurance applications. He approached the task not with irritation or frustration but with the unending, quiet love of a father.

I remember, on many occasions, entering a room in which my father was sitting alone and feeling an aura of peace and love radiating from him. He might have been working on papers or studying a book, yet there was always a tranquil energy in the room. I often wondered how a person could emanate such peace.

Those who met my father seemed to appreciate his loving nature, too. He looked for and found the best in others, and they felt it. People who were shown little unconditional love in their lives often found it in my father.

Even after he had been retired from medicine for a number of years, I continued to encounter his former patients who told me how my father had touched their hearts. One such patient talked about the deep feelings he developed for my father at the age of six while he awaited surgery for an injured eye. It's hard to understand what my father did for this young boy that made such a lasting impression. I can only imagine it had something to do with his warm smile, kind eyes, and loving energy.

It is difficult for me to describe the love I feel for my father. When I think of him, a host of words come to mind—words like smiling, caring, gentle, loving, and giving. Before his eightieth birthday, he wrote these prophetic words to me in a birthday card:

> *Time passes by but still we are vibrant.*
> *Son, enjoy your life with your love, Raye Ann,*
> *and your beautiful kids, Suzanne and David.*
> *This is the pillar of wisdom:*
> *we build for Joy and Everlasting Happiness.*

Truer words were never spoken.

In every moment, every circumstance, every life experience
Opportunities abound

CHAPTER 32

Empower Yourself and Others

C liff, the former Vietnam pilot we met in chapter 9, takes disadvantaged children and teenagers skiing. On one trip, he skied with Andre, a blind high school student. Since Andre had done some skiing before, Cliff took him to a fairly challenging mountain, wanting to give him an opportunity to unleash his potential.

As they began to ski, Cliff would periodically close his eyes, trying to imagine what it was like to ski blind. When he did so, he would focus his attention on his hearing. The most important thing to listen for was snowmobiles, but even if he or Andre heard them, it didn't necessarily follow that the snowmobilers would see them. Cliff's experiment made him realize just how much trust Andre had placed in him and that, unlike this student, he only had to open his eyes to regain his sight.

When Cliff and Andre skied down the mountainside, they performed as a duet, having developed a special communication through their rhythmic movements ... often becoming one another's shadow. And just as Cliff had given Andre the opportunity to experience his unlimited potential, he had also empowered himself by renewing his appreciation for the gift of sight.

On another occasion, Cliff went skiing with Joel, a child with Down syndrome. Although Cliff had been advised to proceed cautiously as he taught Joel to ski, he decided early on that he would give him a lot of independence. Rather than holding him back, he allowed the young skier to have as much freedom as possible.

Joel skied adventurously and left the mountain uttering one word. "Wow!"

On his next outing, Cliff skied with Charlie, a child savant. Charlie had memorized the dictionary up to page 1350 but was unable to put on his ski boots. Instead of fastening the boy's boots for him, Cliff took his own off and had Charlie copy him, step by step, as they put their boots on together.

As Cliff shared these stories with me, I realized his world was one without limits.

PART VII

Staying Connected through Adversity

Pain is felt
Suffering is remembered

—*Sue Mayer*

CHAPTER 33

Pain Is Not Suffering

*P*ain and suffering are not synonymous. Pain is the actual unpleasant sensation we feel when we experience an injury. Suffering, on the other hand, is dependent on how we choose to view the experience. While pain is objective, suffering is subjective. We all experience pain, but our degree of suffering is largely determined by how spiritually connected or centered we are.

If you break a hand, the injury itself is painful. How much you suffer is determined by how you choose to interpret the circumstances surrounding the break. If you injure your hand by being careless, for example, you may criticize yourself repeatedly and suffer significantly. If, however, the hand injury occurs while saving someone's life, your suffering may be inconsequential.

In a nonphysical situation, the distinction between pain and suffering may not be as clear. Let's say that a close friend has a bad accident. You feel pain when you learn of the accident, or when you sense your friend's discomfort, but the suffering you experience depends on how you view life and the degree of peace you feel within. As you become more connected spiritually and come to see meaning and opportunity in every life circumstance, your trust in spiritual love increases and your suffering decreases. You also realize that the peace you feel within, the peace that you radiate, affects others; you understand that your peace can help your friend to quiet his fears and to spiritually reconnect, thereby limiting his suffering and promoting his healing.

While we may feel pain at different times throughout our lives, our level of suffering diminishes as we become more spiritually centered. Actions or events that once might have disturbed us on a superficial level are tempered by our feelings of peace on a deeper level. The pain we experience may also diminish as our emotional state alters our perception of physical discomfort.

Eastern philosophies suggest that suffering ends when we are no longer emotionally attached to specific outcomes. As long as we have certain expectations of how events in our lives will unfold, we are unable to find true peace because the outcome of these events is beyond our control. When we come to accept the experiences that life brings forth, and to trust that within each of these experiences there is beauty and meaning, our suffering lessens significantly. Our experience becomes a part of the natural ebb and flow of life. We come to understand that, in the end, *our lives are largely defined by the peace we feel within.*

☙

Sue delivered her son, Chad, about twenty-five years ago. He was born with Down syndrome. She had a three-year-old at the time and had not been aware of any complications during her second pregnancy. Chad was born at a time when our understanding of Down syndrome was limited. After his birth, Sue's nurse advised her to place him in an institution so he would not interfere with the upbringing of her older son. The nurse's suggestion, which Sue could not take seriously, served only to remind her of the love she felt for this baby.

The first six months were difficult. Sue wasn't sure what to expect, and her support network was small. She and her husband lived in a large city away from family and friends, and they felt apprehensive about the future.

During those early months, Sue's worries limited her ability to relax and experience the true joy of motherhood. She was afraid that she would miss opportunities to stimulate Chad, but when she did take advantage of such opportunities, he achieved milestones that were met with great joy. Even Chad's smallest accomplishments brought tremendous feelings of appreciation. Eventually, Sue's fears began to dissipate, and she was able to enjoy fully the special bond that existed between her and her son. Chad's wonderful spiritual qualities, his innocence and purity, caused her to feel even more blessed.

༄

Like Sue, we all encounter fear on a variety of levels. These fears often interfere with our ability to love, or to truly revel in love, free from worry.

Sue believes that her initial suffering was tied to three fears: a fear of the unknown (how her son's future would unfold), a fear of failure (that she would somehow fall short as a special-needs parent), and a fear of the hardships her son might endure. Her concerns were magnified by well-meaning but misguided health care workers and educators who said such things as, "Your child will stop learning in the sixth grade."

༄

I was given the opportunity to talk with Chad, now in his early twenties, shortly after hearing Sue's story. I wanted to better understand the thoughts and feelings of this young man who appeared to possess such a deep understanding of spirituality.

Our conversation began by my asking Chad what advice he would offer to parents of special-needs kids. He said, "These parents need to express their love for their children by giving them lots of hugs and kisses and telling them they love them as often as possible." He went on to say that parents of special-needs kids should encourage them to achieve their own goals. "Children," he stated, "need to be taught to follow their dreams and reach for the stars!"

Chad praised his teacher for inspiring students like himself to succeed, stating, "We must live life to the fullest and seize the day!" He also expressed great appreciation for all the love and support his parents had shown him.

I asked Chad if he could share some of his spiritual thoughts and beliefs with me. He began by telling me how lucky he was to have so many wonderful people in his life. He was thankful to be living on this earth, and he felt fortunate to have developed so many close relationships.

When I asked Chad what experiences made him feel closest to God, he said that when he helped with communion as a Eucharist minister and when he prayed at night, he felt intimately connected with God. "God's love extends to everyone," he stated, "no matter what course each of us chooses. This most powerful God never stops loving us and never gets angry with us."

When I inquired as to what made him happiest, Chad said it was "talking to other people and making them feel good inside." He went on to say, "We should not judge people on the basis of their skin color, the way they look, or the way they talk." He described the hurt he felt when kids teased him about talking differently. He also told me he felt saddest when he felt he wasn't needed. This usually happened when he was in situations in which he couldn't connect with other people. During such times, he found it beneficial to talk to someone else or to God.

At the end of our evening together, I couldn't help but feel privileged to have spoken with such a loving and inspiring human being. His wisdom seemed to transcend his years, and his angelic heart touched my soul.

I was always confused about why Jesus said "God, why have you forsaken me" if he knew where he came from, where he was going, and why. Why would he have to ask such a question? But then I wonder if it was his human side feeling the pain and fear, which led to a moment of doubt. And then I wonder if he had to experience the same fears and doubts that we all experience so that we can better relate to him and know that he was like us, at least in that way, and that we, too, may someday be like him. And I wonder if the lesson is that doubting is good, as opposed to blind acceptance and blind faith, i.e., that we all need to work through our own pain and fears and doubts to truly believe. And that is when we begin to approach purity.

—Sue Vonderhaar

After writing Chad's story, I met someone who provided a different perspective on suffering.

Joseph, a middle-aged entrepreneur and former Ivy League football player, learned to be independent and responsible at a young age. Ever since he was a child, Joseph had been taught that the secret to success was hard work. He labored at two jobs in the summer and one during the school year as he also strove for academic excellence. In college, if he wasn't studying or practicing football, he was second-guessing past decisions he had made and actions he had undertaken ... continuously wondering if he could have done something better.

Several years ago, Joseph attended a religious speaking engagement. Pat, an old college teammate and friend, was giving the talk. Joseph had always been inspired by Pat's character and passion on the football field, and now Pat's interest had taken a spiritual turn.

Although Joseph was raised Catholic and attended church weekly, his observance was more a result of his strict upbringing than his faith. As he listened to Pat open his heart to the audience that evening, however, Joseph was touched by the peace and joy radiating from his friend.

Joseph suddenly turned to the man on his left and declared, "I want what he has!"

Driving home that night, Joseph reflected on the evening and the difficult challenges in his life. After searching his heart, he decided it was time to let go. As Joseph finally surrendered himself to God, uncontrollable tears coursed down his face. With the release came an overwhelming feeling of love, lifting him up and filling him with joy. Even today, Joseph can't speak of that evening without choking up, his contorted face and moistened eyes conveying the depth of his experience.

Joseph and his wife, Mia, have a daughter, Sabrina, who struggles with an eating disorder, as well as alcohol and drug abuse. Sabrina is in her midtwenties and no longer lives at home, but she calls her parents frequently and becomes upset if they do not respond to her immediate demands. These calls often come in the early morning hours when she finds herself under the effect of alcohol or drugs and needs a ride, a place to sleep, or is in the midst of some other crisis. During these times, she becomes confrontational and tries to influence her parents through guilt and fear.

At other times, when Sabrina is able to reconnect with her inner spirit, her innate beauty and childlike nature rise to the surface. A smile lights her face as she reveals her playful and vulnerable side. She becomes animated, lighthearted, and loving, the sweet little girl Joseph and Mia have always cherished, the one who gets excited about buttery croissants and vanilla milkshakes, the one who is always concerned about others.

Joseph takes his role as provider and protector seriously, and when his daughter slips, it pains him to see her make such unhealthy and dangerous choices, yet his overwhelming need to take care of Sabrina is tempered by his desire to encourage her independence. While he doesn't want to enable Sabrina in her present lifestyle, he recognizes that her life choices are beyond his control.

Joseph's faith has led him to believe that, in time, his daughter will be fine. As such, he has decided to leave the matter in God's hands. He knows that in the long run the lessons learned from Sabrina's experiences will be of great value to everyone in the family, but he still misses his innocent little girl and continues to struggle with his inability to make everything right. It is a struggle that brings him closer to God—one that encourages him to release his fears, to step out with love and faith.

Joseph talks of suffering ... of sacrifice, surrender, and walking with Christ. The suffering of which he speaks is born of meaningful challenges that provide us with the opportunity to lean on God—to let go of our desire to control. It is an unquenchable thirst, or hunger, to commune with the light of love—to quietly surrender amid faith, love, and peace, and the knowledge that God's presence is ever near.

Grief is like a bad houseguest
That doesn't know when to leave

—Julie Backscheider

CHAPTER 34

Grief Is a Feeling of Separation from Love

I can't imagine writing about spirituality without trying to express some words or thoughts of comfort for those who grieve. I lost my father a number of years ago, and I have counseled many others who have experienced such a loss. It can be a heart-wrenching ordeal.

Losing a loved one often presents two challenges. One is dealing with the grief itself. The other is trying to understand why the loss occurred. What possible reason can there be for exposing ourselves to such pain and suffering?

ॐ

Aubrey Rose died on November 10, 2000, just shy of her third birthday. As Aubrey was going through a series of open-heart surgeries, I saw George, her grandfather, in my office periodically for various health issues. Aubrey was always a topic in our conversations. Her grandparents were so enamored with this little girl who was fluent in nonverbal communication. At a moment's notice, these loving grandparents would travel wherever necessary to offer their support for Aubrey and her parents. They spent weeks at a time at different children's hospitals, often staying at Ronald McDonald houses.

As George and I talked, he often shed tears as he spoke about her with hope and empathy. He was so inspired by his granddaughter's strength. No matter the circumstance, Aubrey always wore a smile. She loved life, and she loved to share. If she had a cookie, you had a cookie.

Aubrey's sudden death following a seemingly successful heart and double-lung transplant operation devastated the family. How could they lose this wonderful gift from God?

After Aubrey's passing, her parents decided to establish the Aubrey Rose Foundation to help other children with heart problems. Aubrey's grandmother tells me that as her grandchildren have grown older, many of them have volunteered at the Ronald McDonald house. This brings her great joy.

About two weeks before Christmas in 2003, Aubrey's grandmother, Nancy, came to see me. I could feel her sorrow as she entered my office, but her grief was entwined with beautiful memories and tender thoughts. Nancy told me that after three years, Aubrey's parents still weren't able to do anything to her room, and that hardly a day went by when she herself didn't think of Aubrey, often with tears.

Aubrey's grandparents also spoke of continuing to feel her presence. Often, in the middle of the night, Aubrey's music box would begin to play even though it hadn't been wound. Nancy said she was reluctant to tell people about this for fear they would think she was too imaginative.

It is difficult for many of us to accept the idea that we can continue to experience another's presence long after they have physically left this earth, but it's obvious to me that Aubrey Rose is quite alive in her family's household. At the annual golf outing established in her memory, it's hard not to feel Aubrey's light-filled energy pervading the course as her beautiful nature continues to bring music into the hearts of those she so dearly loved, and her foundation continues to bring hope to those in need through its Healing the World's Hearts Program.

My friend Julie wrote the passage that appears at the top of this chapter. At the age of twenty-three, she lost her mother. Even though her death occurred thirteen years ago, Julie continues to struggle with that loss. She describes her grief as nonlinear in the sense that at any given time it can return full circle, the pain as searing and raw as if her mother had died just yesterday. During these times, the intensity of that grief is surprising to Julie. It is worse during holidays such as Christmas and Mother's Day, though over time, the length of these periods of grief have become shorter and shorter.

Julie says it's important for people to realize that they may continue to grieve for the rest of their lives and that this can be a normal part of such an experience. She believes that people who have suffered a loss need to give themselves permission to grieve, even after a long period of time.

A few years ago, Julie shared her experience with me. After telling me her story, I asked Julie to write it down so I might share it with others:

> I've needed my mother many, many times over the last eleven years, but she has never been there, except in my mind. Her death was the making of me. We're different, those of us whose mothers have gone and left us to fend for ourselves. On some deep emotional level, we are on our own. "No girl becomes a woman until her mother dies," goes an old proverb. My mother's greatest calling was me, and when she passed away, I became an adult overnight. This makes some of us hard, sometimes angry and driven, too. We perform with courage on a stage in front of an empty audience—look at me, Mom, I'm fine, I did okay.
>
> My son, Jack, is an exceptional ball player. Unfortunately, my mother has never had the chance to meet him; she passed away two years before he was

born. The other day at his game, my son hit a home run, and I imagined I heard the sound of two hands clapping. The two that aren't there. The only ones that count.

My mother was the only person who ever loved me unconditionally, and her death has left a hole in my heart and nothing to plug it. The grief inside does seem a little better when we who have lost our mothers become mothers ourselves.

My children do not understand what it feels like, what has happened to me, and I hope they never will. I know someday they will lose me, but I hope it is when they have years of not only my love but the love of their own spouses and children and the knowledge that they have learned everything I have to teach. I never had that. When my mother died, I was young and too young to live my life without her. Things will be all right but never the same. When your mother dies, you never get used to it. You always want her back.

I've learned a lot with my mother's death—about being a good person and a loving mother. I am a strong person now, but I would trade all I have learned for what I lost so long ago.

Until recently, Julie harbored a great deal of anger toward God over the loss of her mother. She felt cheated that so many of her friends still had their mothers and that she was unable to share the everyday things in life that they still could. At that time, she read *When Bad Things Happen to Good People*, by Harold S. Kushner, and felt her anger begin to recede. She began to realize that God was not responsible for her mother's death. With further spiritual reading, Julie gradually came to understand that everyone's problems are unique and started to focus on the positives in her life.

Two years after telling me her story, Julie shared the following:

> It has been thirteen years since my mother's death, and the bitterness has been eating at my soul, making me the person my mom would not have wanted me to be.
>
> I now have a peaceful sadness, if that makes any sense. I realize that I cannot think of what I would have had with my mom. Instead I have learned to cherish what I did have. All I have to do is close my eyes and the memories are right there. I remember the long talks on our front porch, working on word searches, her dry meatloaf, and playing bingo on Thursday evenings.
>
> I regret the bitterness I had for so many years. I am finally at peace with my mom's passing. I thank you, God, for what you gave me: the gift of being a daughter and the twenty-three years I was able to spend with a loving, devoted person. At last, my soul has taken a deep breath of life, and it sure feels wonderful to have the pain lifted from me after all of these years.

Julie noticed the difference this past Mother's Day. In previous years, she had always felt melancholic on Mother's Day. Her children had often wondered what was wrong, but, for Julie, the day was one of mourning. This year, however, things were different. She happily spent the day with her children and husband, enjoying and relishing her own experience as a mother … understanding that this was, in fact, the best way to pay tribute to her mom.

Natalie lost an aunt to whom she was especially close. This is her story:

> One night I was sitting in my son's bedroom feeling very sad, crying as I rocked him. I missed my aunt terribly, and waves of sadness seemed to wash over me unexpectedly. As I rocked in the chair, I suddenly felt my aunt's presence fill the room and communicate to me that she was all right, that there was no need for me to cry. I felt an immediate sense of relief—and great peace.
>
> Later, as I shared this story with my aunt's daughter, Lori, I learned that she had also been grieving that night. To my surprise, Lori told me that her mother had also visited her with the very same communication at the very same time. As she told me this, I felt a chill run up my spine. I had never realized that those who have died communicate with us.

❧

I lost my father in the summer of 2004. He had been hospitalized for recurrent heart problems and died following a three-hour cardiac procedure that had been considered routine. Nonetheless, it was not totally unexpected; several weeks earlier, my wife had shared with me a feeling she'd had that my father would be dying soon.

I remember driving him to the hospital—the one in which he would die, smiling at him as I tousled his hair, telling him, "You've been such a wonderful dad!"

He looked back at me and with a tender smile said, "I'm not dying, George."

"I know," I replied.

I was fortunate to have had the opportunity to spend some quiet time with him in the hospital before he died. On two separate occasions, as I helped him get comfortable for the night, I experienced a strong and extended feeling of serene peace. During this time, I also came to feel that my father was at peace with his life and the prospect of death.

Immediately after my father's passing, I went into the cardiac procedure room in which he had died and tried to feel his spirit. Before I could establish a connection with him, however, the rest of my family came in and began grieving. It was a challenging night as I witnessed my brother's and mother's raw, inconsolable pain.

Later that evening, when I was once again by myself, I tried to reconnect with my father's spirit as I drove home in my open convertible. As my mind grew quiet, I began to feel his presence in a manner I had never expected. Looking up at the dark gray-blue sky, softened by clouds, I began to feel his presence through the beautiful night surroundings. I felt him in the sky, as well as in the gently swaying trees, and through the songs of the crickets in the surrounding woods. I came to realize that my father's spirit, like God's, was everywhere. I needed only to quiet my mind and be receptive to it.

I remember finding it difficult to wear dark clothing on the day of his funeral. The dark clothes spoke more of my father's death than of a celebration of his life and his transition into spirit.

Although in the following weeks I quietly reflected on my father's passing by listening to soft music and visiting the cemetery daily, my focus was on communing with his ongoing presence. During this period, I became excited at the prospect of being spiritually guided by my father. Since his death, I have felt a stronger and more persistent connection with spiritual love than ever before.

I would like to end this chapter with an excerpt from a poem that reflects my feelings about my father's passing:

Do not stand at my grave and weep,
I am not there; I do not sleep.
I am a thousand winds that blow,
I am the diamond's glint on snow.

I am the sunlight on ripening grain,
I am the gentle autumn's rain.
Do not stand at my grave and cry,
I am not there; I did not die.

—Mary Frye (attributed)

Dad, I love you.

A silent blessing of love
To all in our path
For when we look deeply
We see a reflection of ourselves
In everyone we encounter

CHAPTER 35

Forgiveness Is Love

Heather spent three years living with her stepfather, John, who was physically abusive. John would beat her mother with anything that was readily available, including a wooden club. On one occasion, he broke her arm. Heather still remembers seeing her mother being dragged across the floor by her hair after she had refused to accept his apology. John was also physically abusive with her younger brother, Nick, whom he whipped with a belt. He beat Heather as well.

Heather's half sister, Trish, who was several years younger than Heather, never saw this side of her father. She idolized him. One day, as seven-year-old Trish was talking about her love for her father, Heather, then twelve years old, shouted, "Your dad's a monster!" Trish didn't believe her.

Heather's mom divorced John a short time later. After several years, Trish learned the truth about her father, who by then wanted to make amends with his stepchildren. John asked Trish repeatedly to tell Heather that he thought of her and Nick often and that he was sorry about the way he had treated them. Trish did what he asked of her, but Heather wanted nothing to do with him.

A number of years later, John's mother died. Trish had been exceptionally close to her grandmother and needed the support of her family to help her cope with her grandmother's passing, but Heather had reservations about going to the funeral. She had no interest in seeing John. She'd had no contact with him since he and her mother had divorced, yet she knew she needed to be there for Trish.

On the morning of the funeral, Heather felt nauseated and sweaty. Her heart was racing. It was the way she felt when she'd taken in too much caffeine without enough food—the feeling she would get when her brain told her "this is not good."

Later that day as Heather entered the church, she felt lightheaded and jittery. She didn't really know how to act, but she didn't want to appear nervous. Once inside, she thought she saw John out of the corner of her eye, but she tried not to look in his direction. She was unsure of how she might respond. Then she saw her mother and Trish walk past John without acknowledging him. When they stopped to talk to her aunt, Heather started to relax, knowing she could just join them. As she turned around to approach their group, though, she found John standing a few feet in front of her.

Heather made eye contact with John and moved closer to him. He looked different from what she remembered. Gone was the big, mean, aggressive stepfather; in his place was an old and vulnerable man, overweight and gray. She could feel his sadness and despair. Her heart went out to him. With little forethought, Heather reached out to embrace him. As she wrapped her arms around him and expressed her sorrow about his mother's passing, he began to cry.

When Heather rejoined her family, she was met with ugly looks that spoke of betrayal.

"Why did you hug him?" her mother asked.

"I'm vulnerable, I'm in a church," Heather said, in an attempt at lighthearted humor. "He's upset; he just lost his mother."

"You didn't have to hug him," her mother replied bitterly. "That's what he expects, that we will forget about all the things he did."

After the service, John came over and put his hand on Heather's mother's shoulder, shook hands with another family member, and thanked them for coming. Heather's mother refused to look at him.

For the next few days, Heather wondered whether she had done the right thing. After all, she was no longer the abused girl of her youth. She was on her own now and had grown spiritually. Yet she had been raised to be loyal to the family. Family was always supposed to come first; it was family you could trust. She had always listened to her mother—bowed to her wishes—but this time she hadn't. Had she betrayed her family by hugging John and extending love to him?

At church the following Sunday, the sermon's topic was "The Truth about Love." The preacher began by asking, "What did Jesus say about love?" He went on to say, "Our society talks about getting even and doing something back, but love isn't about getting even. It's easy to love people who love you. But Jesus said we should love everyone. Pray for your enemies. Love them anyway."

As she listened to the sermon, Heather knew she had done the right thing. She felt a sense of peace and a release of past resentments. She didn't believe it was by chance that her reunion with John had taken place in a church. Although Heather was surprised that she had been able to extend love to John, she understood that her actions arose not from her mind but from her heart. She also came to realize that her experience had nothing do to with her mother, her sister, or even John. It was a healing experience—a loving experience—between herself and God.

As opportunities arise
Each of us must ask ourselves
"Who am I?"

CHAPTER 36

Be True to Yourself

A re we living our lives in a way that is true to our hearts? Are we seizing the opportunities made available to us to help us realize our potential? Are we taking advantage of our intrinsic talents?

These are all difficult but important considerations that can help each of us to answer the following question:

Am I living my life to the fullest?

ॐ

A number of years ago, I was asked to give a series of presentations on post traumatic stress disorder. The circumstances surrounding the talks were very inviting: the background material and slides for the talks had already been prepared; I found the subject matter interesting; and I would receive reasonable compensation for my time while strengthening my skills at public speaking. Although I had never felt comfortable with public speaking and could never have imagined myself voluntarily entering this arena, I felt a strange desire to undertake this challenge. I couldn't exactly define the feeling at the time, but it was one of underlying excitement intermixed with fear, a feeling of both empowerment and uncertainty. I was reminded of a time at summer camp when I was eight years old, sick, and in need of an injection. I had always been scared to death of shots, but for some reason on that day I felt drawn to the challenge. Likewise, I found myself unexpectedly drawn toward this opportunity.

My initial expectations were not great. I merely wanted to be able to give the presentations without feeling unduly anxious, or at least not to project my nervousness to the audience and to relay the information in a professional manner. On the night of my first talk, I felt like a seven-year-old boy standing on a ten-foot diving board: feeling up so very high, looking down at the water that seemed so far away, grateful that my nervousness wasn't readily apparent.

Shortly after this initial speaking engagement, I traveled to Arizona for a weekend-long speaker-training seminar. On my flight out, I reviewed the information that I was to present. That night, immediately following an outdoor dinner set amid the majesty of the arid desert and surrounding mountains, all of the participants had to give talks, which were videotaped. After the talks, we were critically evaluated by a group of professional speakers who were merciless.

Throughout the entire weekend, we gave presentations on various subjects with minimal time for preparation. These talks were followed by honest, oftentimes harsh, feedback from the instructors. But on some level, I knew they deeply wanted us to succeed, to foster in us their passion for excellence. Although the weekend proved to be stressful, I was amazed at how much I learned. As I reflect on the training, I believe it is similar to the way soldiers often feel about their experience at boot camp; I didn't particularly relish my time there, but I came out feeling stronger and more prepared for the future.

I was eventually asked to present more talks on a variety of subjects. As my confidence grew, I began to view speaking more from the standpoint of the listener. My focus became centered on keeping the listener interested and, I hoped, somewhat entertained. I found that I enjoyed my talks most when they were interactive. I especially liked giving talks on depression, as these discussions seemed to take place on another level. Although I failed to realize it at the time, I now believe that level was spiritual.

During these sessions on depression, which often involved a small number of professionals, a sense of community would develop. As I interacted with doctors and nurses in an intimate setting, we moved beyond the boundaries of traditional medicine. The energy was heightened as we talked about the human spirit—about the pain of individuals who struggle with depression and about reaching out to them with love. It was a quiet yet excited energy—one of understanding, hope, and empowerment. God was present in all of his wonder, but as someone who at the time was unsure of his existence, I was only aware that *something* was different and that it felt good.

Although I initially felt challenged with public speaking, I never would have experienced this meaningful undertaking if I hadn't been willing to step outside of my comfort zone. Now, as I write about spirituality, I wonder if at some point I will be speaking on this subject as well—encouraging others to share their spiritual thoughts and experiences with one another in a setting of love and intimacy. If so, perhaps my opportunity to become a better public speaker was not as accidental as I once thought.

Success is not the key to happiness
Happiness is the key to success
If you love what you are doing
You will be successful

—*Albert Schweitzer*

At times, we all find ourselves in situations where it is easier to flow with the current than to try to swim upstream. It's easier to do what others expect of us than to expend the energy it would require to go in a different direction. Perhaps we are reluctant to move in those directions because we feel that others may not understand our actions. In any event, if we choose to act in ways that reflect our true nature, we will foster feelings of peace and joy. Just as acting in non-loving ways distances us from feeling connected with God, acting in ways that are not true to ourselves leads us away from self-love, away from the heightened energy of passion and self-expression.

I left my medical practice in August 2007, having made the decision to retire earlier that year. I had little to no financial security, but I knew God was calling me. For several years, I had practiced medicine unconventionally: spending an extended amount of time with individual patients; reaching out to others in meaningful ways while being open to their teachings; taking long lunch hours to write or engage in spiritual discussions; living life to the fullest.

I knew I could not accomplish all of my goals if I continued in my practice. Although I thoroughly enjoyed taking care of patients (many of whom I thought of as friends), especially when I could use spirituality as a tool to ease their anxiety or depression, I felt the need to devote myself entirely to writing and other spiritual endeavors.

One of the hardest challenges I faced was dealing with the resistance I encountered from family and friends with regard to the path I had chosen. Their concerns were genuine. It was hard for them to understand my spiritual calling. With a daughter going to college soon, little financial security, and a significant mortgage payment, my choices didn't make sense to them. Why couldn't I simply continue to practice medicine while I worked on my book? After all, the financial prospects for a first-time author were very uncertain.

However, I knew that I needed to step out onto the water, to move boldly. God was calling me, and I was listening. What others didn't understand was that by continuing to practice medicine, even part-time, I was closing off other options.

Over time, I found God encouraging me to step out even further into the unknown with blind faith. He was reminding me to live my life from the perspective of abundance and to seize the day. This is what he conveyed to me through my son, David, who receives spiritual communications.

When you live abundantly, although you have nothing, you show the amount of faith you really have. In the midst of all confusion, there is clarity. In the midst of all that is dark, there is light. In the midst of all that is fear, there is love.

And so I have chosen to walk even farther out onto the water, holding his hand ever so tightly, with a new level of trust that would not otherwise have been possible. But if I stumble and fall, I know that I am not alone. At the very least, I will have tried.

Yet I know in my heart that I have already realized my dreams, for I have come to understand that this path is not about distant outcomes but rather about overcoming the limits I have placed upon myself. And so I give thanks for the opportunity of a lifetime, for his ever-present guidance and love, and for the unwavering faith he has in me and in each one of us.

As we move forward in search of the light
We slowly discover our majestic beauty

CHAPTER 37

Courage Enables Us to Soar

This topic touches my heart more than any other. I see so many people who have encountered an array of difficult obstacles but somehow continue to move forward. They may have lost someone who truly brought them joy. They may feel their lives lack meaning or purpose, or they may feel overwhelmed by their present life circumstances.

Yet these people still manage to go on. They don't realize that so many others are facing similar challenges. They feel so lost, alone, and hopeless that they often are unable to see the beauty in themselves; this, in itself, speaks of their humility. Such vulnerability and childlike innocence imbues in me a tremendous love for the human spirit. In these circumstances, it is easy to see a part of God in each of us. Our ability to continually search for the light, no matter how faint, is courage.

☙

I noticed how beautiful she was from the first time I saw her. I am not simply talking about outward beauty but the purity of spirit that a person radiates from deep within. Ellen was in her late forties but could easily have passed for her midthirties. Her voice was soft, her eyes kind. There was a gentleness there, as if a delicate flower were growing amid rocky terrain, amid the challenges of everyday living. Her mother had committed suicide when she was twelve. Her sister and father had died when she was forty-one.

Ellen had endured a challenging marriage in which she felt pressured to conform, to become someone she wasn't. Despite her best efforts, the marriage didn't survive. She was supposed to be a hot, forty-something mother—the mother who always looked ravishing, the mother who was too cool. Except that wasn't who she was. She was more like a birch tree in midgrowth, her bark smooth and layered, her branches full of leaves and life, swaying in the wind, leaning toward the sun—the light—with vulnerability and strength. Perhaps not as striking as a Japanese maple but richer, more textured.

As Ellen became clear on who she wasn't, she also began to discover who she was. Having found and recently married her soul mate, Ellen was coming into her own. Like many mothers, her kids had always come first; she was a natural-born nurturer. In the process of raising her children, however, there had been little time for self-reflection. She had always spoken softly and encouragingly to her kids. While trying to give them the love and freedom to grow, she would also radiate truth. She would allow them to see how their words and actions affected her; like a mirror, her face would simply reflect what was said. No guilt, no control—simply truth. Words of love created a smile, hostile words pain.

Now her son, Kellen, was struggling. He was the son who had always been sensitive and lighthearted, who would befriend the person sitting alone in the school cafeteria, who at age fourteen would still affectionately sit on her lap. A student at Ohio State, he had begun to skip classes, to get high on marijuana, and to develop paranoid delusions. "They" were after him, following him around, trying to control his thoughts and actions. He could trust very few.

After picking up Kellen from school and bringing him home, Ellen simply listened to him. She was cautious not to spur his defenses, not to become placed in the group he didn't trust—an increasingly large group that now included almost everyone. But aside from extending love, she didn't know what to do. She had always radiated truth, except her truth was no longer his.

As I talked with Ellen during this period, she appeared distraught. Like many parents, nothing unnerved her more than watching her child suffer. She was at a loss as to how to reach Kellen, how to cope. He was on an emotional roller coaster, and she was sitting next to him. Up, down, up, down—the ride was becoming agonizing.

And so, she had begun to ask herself, "What is the opportunity for me in this situation?"

The answer, she discovered, lay inside of her—by going inward, becoming still, and finding peace. Once reconnected, she could then help her son; she could radiate unencumbered love and light.

To learn more about her son's illness, Ellen initially felt guided toward the Internet. As she studied the information there, she came to discover more about the world her son was living in. It was a world of uncertainty and distrust, a world of despair. She knew Kellen needed help, so she sought out a psychiatrist. For a period of several weeks, while he was still in Columbus at Ohio State, she would drive the two hours from Cincinnati to pick him up after school so that he would be home in time for an 8:30 p.m. appointment. The next morning, she would leave at 3:00 a.m. to drop him off at Ohio State and be back in Cincinnati by 8:00 a.m. for work. She would do this two to three times a week, just so Kellen could stay in school and experience some degree of normalcy. Eventually, however, he left Ohio State and came home to live.

The more time Kellen spent with Ellen, the more he came to see her as one of "them"—someone he couldn't trust. He would call the police on her, accusing her of all sorts of things. She was, after all, trying to poison him. The police would arrive at the house, and after spending time questioning Kellen, would gain an appreciation for what this mother and son were going through—a world turned upside down.

In keeping with his paranoia, Kellen became increasingly

distrustful of his doctor and his medication. He was adrift and, without his medicine, began moving further out to sea. He would seldom look anyone in the eye. He would take several minutes before responding to a question, his mind overloaded with noise.

As a means to better understand and cope, Ellen visited support groups. It was disheartening for her to learn that this type of illness could continue without end, and equally so to see how many other parents were struggling with the same issues she was facing. She was advised to try the philosophy of "tough love": setting boundaries, establishing limits, and having expectations. When she implemented these ideas at home, however, Ellen felt the distance between Kellen and herself widen.

Shortly thereafter, Ellen remembered who she really was—a mother whose hand was eternally extended. She realized that she was unprepared to force Kellen out of the house even if he was unwilling to take his medicine. "Tough love" simply wasn't her truth. As she came to understand this, she came to better understand herself, to see herself in a gentler light.

During this time, Ellen found herself reaching out to God as she never had before. She no longer saw him as a force mainly present at church but as a companion and friend. She was trying to understand—to find comfort and peace. Ellen wanted "God close," right up against her. She would read books, undertake spiritual discussions, and talk with him in the most intimate of manners. She would pray on her knees, with the faith and innocence of a child.

Although she initially tried to control the outcome of events with Kellen, especially after having lost her mentally depressed mother to suicide, Kellen continued to suffer. Ellen no longer knew what to do or how best to help him. She decided to surrender everything to God, to place her trust completely in him. She immediately began to experience the peace for which she had been searching.

On a Friday morning, as I stood on a beach in Siesta Key, Florida, I received a phone call from my office. The call was from Sue, our receptionist and a close friend. Sue, like me, felt a strong affinity for Ellen. We had shared many conversations about the beauty we saw in Ellen and the challenges she was facing. For some time, I had emphasized Sue's and Ellen's similarities: their devotion to family, their purity of heart.

Ever polite, Sue began the conversation by asking about me and my family. "How is Florida?"

"We're having a great time," I said. "The kids are enjoying themselves, and Raye Ann and I are taking a lot of long walks."

"I am glad that you're getting to spend so much quality time together," Sue replied.

After pausing for a second, she said, "George, I have some bad news for you." As the words hung in the air, she went on to say, "Last night Kellen committed suicide."

Startled, I said, "Whaaaat?"

"Yeah, I'm really sorry to have to tell you." Sue continued, "He shot himself."

I felt unbalanced, uneasy. "What happened?" I wondered.

Then slowly, I came to understand. The pain and confusion had become too much. Kellen had released himself.

After the news had sunk in, I started to re-center myself and to feel more peaceful. My thoughts turned to Ellen.

"How is Ellen doing?"

Sue was uncertain. She only knew that as a mother, she couldn't imagine dealing with something so painful. I could sense her compassion, her worry. After talking to Sue for a little while, I told her I would call Ellen when I felt the moment was right. I would take some time to process the events and give Ellen some time as well. Spirit would let me know when to call.

Later that day, I stood out on the beach as dusk approached, took a moment to commune with God, and made the call. As I spoke with Ellen, I could feel a deep sadness within her. She was grieving for her son, but at the same time, I could also sense her strength and understanding. She spoke of Kellen's constant struggles, his irrational behavior, and the pain of watching him slowly wither and turn into a shell of his former self. Now his suffering was over. He had returned home.

As I talked with Ellen, I was surprised to find myself connecting with Kellen's energy in the most positive of manners. I had always been taught that when people commit suicide they enter a state of limbo, a state not connected with peace, but this was not what I was sensing.

Kellen seemed to be in a joyful state, at one with spirit. I could feel him soaring, welling with love. In the absence of his mental illness, he had returned to his former self—someone deeply connected to others and filled with light. I couldn't help but wonder if all the love he had extended to family and friends throughout his life was now coming back to him and helping him to heal. As I looked up, I noticed the sun beginning to set. Under the deep blue evening sky, accented with silky white clouds, the gulls called to one another in their encouraging high-pitched tones, the waves rolled softly in to shore, and a peacefulness resonated within me. I felt uplifted.

When I shared my thoughts with Ellen, I was happy to hear that she, too, had a similar feeling. She sensed that Kellen was gliding with peace. We both knew that in the coming days she would experience emotional fluctuations, but her energy was rising. It was time for her to release her fears and embrace love. Kellen was soaring, and now she could as well.

I didn't talk to Ellen again until the visitation. As I entered the funeral home and laid eyes on her, I was taken aback. She exuded an energy unlike any I had ever seen. She simply radiated light ... like a candle in a darkened church. Her expression was devoid of fear, of sadness. It reflected only peace, the serenity of someone in harmony with themselves and spirit.

Despite a long line of family and friends waiting to extend their condolences—many in their teens and early twenties, attending their first viewing—Ellen took her time with each person. Like an angel sent from heaven, she comforted with pure gentleness.

Kellen was with her in spirit, and together they reached out to others unabashedly, with the openness and tenderness of a child. As each of the mourners approached, she enveloped them in a hug that spoke of reassurance and faith, a hug that completed and restored them. She felt their pain, their confusion. Yet through her warm embrace, their fears melted away. Instead, a heightened energy arose within them, and, with hope-filled eyes, they once again saw the beauty in life.

Later that evening, when I had a chance to ask Ellen how she was coping, she smiled and told me she was soaring. I could feel her peace. Although the days and months ahead would be challenging, I knew she had reached the summit. She had accomplished the unimaginable. On the night of her son's visitation she had become one with the light of God.

Through love
All things are possible

—An expression favored by my daughter, Suzanne

CHAPTER 38

Our Spiritual Journey
Is Just Beginning

O n a summer's eve, I was dining outside at a restaurant in Newport, Kentucky. It was a slightly cool, pleasant evening, and the veranda offered a beautiful view of the Cincinnati skyline. I was working on a story when my server, Nikki, entered the scene.

Nikki was in her late twenties with long brown hair, an inviting smile, and a slightly protruding belly. She was six months' pregnant. I soon discovered that she also had a sixteen-month-old daughter. On a hunch, I asked her whether she had ever had any spiritual experiences as a mother. I went on to explain that by spiritual I didn't mean religious but rather a feeling of being connected with something greater than herself. Nikki told me she was interested in becoming more spiritual but that so far she couldn't recall having had any identifiable experiences.

In an attempt to broaden my question, I asked Nikki if she had experienced anything unusual or extraordinary as a mother. On reflection, she remembered that she had made some significant lifestyle changes after she became pregnant with her first child. When I asked her what had motivated her to make these changes, she said it was a sense of purpose. She *knew* there was something special about what was happening: she was fulfilling a role that was meant to be.

Speaking of her first pregnancy, Nikki went on to tell me that although she had not used birth control for two years, she had been surprised when she became pregnant with her firstborn, as if it had come to be by more than just chance. As I watched her, I could see the wheels turning in her head. She had a peaceful yet reflective look, a look of increased awareness.

I soon discovered that Nikki was reawakening to something deep and long forgotten, something reassuring and astonishing. She was remembering that on some level her life was guided—that there was purpose and meaning in her life's journey, one that she was actively creating. She was also sensing that at some point, perhaps a long time ago, she had *chosen* to experience motherhood.

A little later, as Nikki returned to my table, I noticed her step was lighter, her mood elevated, as if she had just awakened from a delicious dream, one that reminded her of her intimate connection with spirit. I went on to ask her how being a mother had affected her. She told me she couldn't imagine life without her daughter. As we talked further, I inquired about her thoughts on love. She said she was amazed by the power of love, how it takes hold of someone and influences that person beyond measure.

I then asked Nikki about the love she felt for her daughter. What did she feel when she looked at her little girl? She smiled, stared off with a look of quiet serenity, and said, "It's indescribable."

Reflecting further, she excitedly declared, "Love is what it's all about!"

PART VIII

Surrendering to God

During times of inexplicable pain and uncertainty
When all seems lost
We may find comfort in the miracle of love

CHAPTER 39

Somewhere ... A Miracle
Is Unfolding

On October 22, three friends of mine, Ellen, Sue and Barb, arrived in Chicago to witness a miracle. They didn't know what this miracle might entail, but they knew it was to occur on the following day, the twenty-third of October. They also came to welcome my son, David, and me back from an arduous spiritual journey. I had asked for their support during this difficult period, and they had offered it willingly, selflessly. They had been invited through guidance, and, as usual, that guidance would prove to be extraordinary.

During their Chicago visit, we began each meal with a spiritual toast—to love, faith, and the beauty of spirit. As we ate, we shared our most intimate thoughts and experiences in an atmosphere of peace and laughter. There was so much love present, it would have been hard for an outsider not to feel it—the light-filled energy, the easy smiles, the enveloping warmth. It was in this setting that David and I were welcomed back from some of the most challenging experiences of our lives. In the gentle embrace of friends, we were reminded of our strengths, of our ability to help others quiet the noise in their lives and to connect spiritually. These women, or perhaps I should say angels, did not judge or question. On the contrary, their faith in us was absolute.

On the morning of the twenty-third, the five of us set out on a walk around the city. Ellen, who had recently lost her son, felt we should seek out the church whose bells kept calling to her as she lay in her hotel room—a call no one else had heard even though we were all staying at the same establishment. To Ellen, those bells rang sweetly, like a welcoming invitation. And so we began our afternoon looking for the source of those bells, which eventually led us to St. Peter's Church.

We passed through the heavy gold doors and into the dimly lit church. Seeing that a Mass was in progress, we climbed the gray steps to the balcony from which we quietly watched the service. It was hard not to feel the heightened energy from our lofty perch. The parishioners knelt humbly before God—heads lowered, hands clasped, spirit willing. Nothing was held back—love radiated from their souls, appreciation from their hearts.

Later the five of us lit a candle together in the presence of God. It was a quiet, simple, and unifying experience.

During the early evening hours, we strolled through downtown. As the late afternoon rays of the sun began to mingle with the night sky, we drifted toward Lake Michigan and the nearby parks. There was only the slightest hint of a breeze as we marveled at the powerful, symmetrical trees that lined the walkways, their leaves aglow in hues of orange, red, and green, and a multicolored sky that spoke the language of God and love.

Later, as we broke bread together in a softly lit restaurant overlooking Lake Michigan, we spoke of the significance of the October twenty-third date and wondered about the miracle that was to have occurred that day, the one that no one had noticed.

For many months, David and I had sensed that this date would be momentous based on a spiritual communication he had received. I had come to pin many of my hopes and dreams on the miracle that would unfold that day, but now the twenty-third was almost over and there was no tangible evidence that any miracle had taken place.

Ellen was the first to speak. She looked around the table at the four of us, smiled, and said, "I know that somewhere, someplace, a miracle is occurring tonight."

As she spoke, there was a palpable change in the surrounding energy.

No one moved. All was quiet. Time stood still.

As Ellen's words echoed in the stillness, I connected with something greater, something purer.

The universe held out its hand in invitation and whispered, "Believe!"

At that moment, I realized I no longer needed to see the miracle because I knew the statement to be true. I could simply trust that this long-sought-after event was unfolding somewhere, somehow, just as Ellen had said.

On that night, in a setting of love and fellowship, I came to realize that at least two miracles had taken place on the twenty-third.

The first was the one of which Ellen spoke.

The second was of a more personal nature. At that moment, after anticipating the twenty-third of October for almost a year and waiting for this grand, undefined miracle that was inexplicably destined for that date, I simply knew, without any tangible evidence, that it had taken place. I could feel the energy and appreciate the beauty as this realization came over me in a setting of great faith.

From that moment on, my life would never be the same. This experience would take me to an infinitely higher level of trust, and in the days to come, I would rely on that trust unconditionally, venturing forth along my path with blind faith.

Yet I would learn that faith was only one part of the trilogy of life. Without love, and without our individual truths—our individual dreams, faith was no more than an unfertilized seed. It would take all three to bear bountiful fruit.

In the whisper of the spirit
We find the light of love

CHAPTER 40

Beyond the Ephemeral

I met Father Bill through Mary Lou, a patient of mine. Mary Lou had an intuitive feeling that she should get the two of us together over dinner. I had taken care of both her and her recently deceased mother, Lucy, for a long time.

Lucy, who seemed more like a sister than a mother to Mary Lou, died in her early nineties. Despite Lucy's poor health in her latter years, she was never one to miss an outing, never one to stop smiling. At the age of ninety, her heart failure in check, she headed off to Las Vegas with Mary Lou. The two of them were inseparable. Theirs was an attachment formed in heaven; beyond blood, it was one of spirit.

As I entered Mary Lou's house that evening, I handed her a seven-inch oak-stained cross. Attached to its center was a bronze-hued wooden star that spoke of radiating light and love. The delicate cross, suspended from a strand of light brown fabric, reflected beauty and simplicity. I was reminded of an earlier time—of robes and sandals.

Mary Lou introduced me to Father Bill, who was in his late forties, had light-colored hair, and stood well over six feet tall. As he arose to shake my hand, I was struck by his refreshing presence, his unassuming manner.

Mary Lou then asked Father Bill to bless the cross I had given her. As he did so, he held it with great care, as he might a sacred object, and then, with hands raised, began to deliver a prayer. The energy in the room changed markedly. This was no perfunctory blessing. It was one of holiness, of piety. In less than a minute, it was over.

Over the course of the evening, Father Bill spoke of some of his unusual encounters. Mary Lou initiated the discussion, bringing up different stories she had heard and urging him to share them. I learned that Father Bill hadn't entered the priesthood until later in life. He was in his thirties at the time. His biggest surprise was learning how much administrative work would be required of him on a daily basis.

Although I was enjoying our conversation, I remained curious as to why Mary Lou had felt it so important that Father Bill and I meet. As the evening progressed, however, it became clear to me. We were there to exchange spiritual stories and ideas, to learn from each other in a setting of love and brotherhood. He was one more role model, a modern-day Christ, who had answered the call with faith and purity of heart. I would come to discover that Father Bill had been blessed with many gifts that he humbly believed everyone possessed.

I was particularly fascinated to find that Father Bill seemed to operate in a limitless environment, a setting absent of rules. He was obviously familiar with church teachings, but rather than treat those doctrines as an end point, he used them as a beginning.

When I told him about a recent trip David and I had taken to Lake Tahoe and related our interest in achieving the impossible—of literally experiencing heaven on earth—he implicitly understood. I spoke of *a barrier* that existed between heaven and earth, one of which Christ was well aware but of which few others knew, and even fewer had broken.

It required blind faith to break this barrier, a willingness to step out onto the water with certainty. One needed to walk as Christ did, ridding oneself of all doubt and fear, so that the love and light within shone forth unencumbered. It necessitated a complete surrender to God, the ultimate state of spirit. One would have to proceed with the purest of intentions, with unremitting persistence, and with a knowing that life is a series of limitless opportunities. It would be a journey undertaken with abundance, with an embracing of God's unending gifts.

Father Bill was intrigued by this perspective. Although the concept of absolute faith and surrendering to God were not new to him, the idea of piercing this barrier between heaven and earth was.

At that point, Father Bill told me a story about one of his parishioners, Dorothy, who was quite sick. He had gone to visit her in the hospital at the request of her family, who felt it was her time to pass. Upon entering the hospital room, he was at first startled and then intrigued by a beautiful beam of light that he saw next to Dorothy. He had never seen an angel before, but the image was unmistakable. As he spoke to Dorothy, he asked her if she was aware of the angel at her side. She said she was. Her daughter, who sat nearby, was not. Father Bill softly told Dorothy the angel was there to take her home, that it was time to leave. But Dorothy wasn't ready.

After a short stay in the hospital, Dorothy went home, only to return within days. Two weeks later, Father Bill visited her again. This time as he entered the room, he unexpectedly encountered three angels of light. Once more, he asked her if she was aware of their presence, and Dorothy, for a second time, responded in the affirmative. Father Bill explained to her again that the angels were there to take her home. This time, she was ready to go. She died shortly thereafter.

Father Bill went on to tell me that during confession when parishioners came in for solace, he would urge them to let go of past unloving thoughts and actions and become receptive to forgiveness and love. Curiously, though, the unloving behaviors of which he spoke had not always been conveyed to him by his parishioners.

For example, a parishioner might come to confession and mention only his insensitivity toward his spouse. Without going into detail, Father Bill might then begin talking about that parishioner's indiscretions with other women. As he did so, it would be without judgment and in a manner that it would leave the parishioner wondering who had been the one to initiate the discussion.

In these situations, Father Bill was intuitive enough to pick up on the thoughts of others through the guidance of spirit. He was in communion with these parishioners, helping them to release past hurts and to move forward unburdened. By the following day, Father Bill would no longer be able to remember the details of those confessions. There was no need.

Father Bill also described how he would stand at the altar as his parishioners prayed in church. One parishioner might be praying for her grandmother's health, another for the strength and courage to deal with his drug addiction. Even though they never openly expressed their concerns to Father Bill, he intuitively knew the subject of their prayers. He was both surprised and touched to see how closely connected he was with his congregation. Yet it was disturbing for him when he witnessed the loving spirit of God approach one of the parishioners ... only to see that person refuse entry to this loving energy. As spirit left that individual's presence, "it was eerie." God's gentle hand had been rebuffed.

Toward the end of the evening, Mary Lou spoke of how she often felt her deceased mother's presence at church. As she sat in a pew, her mind quiet, she could feel Lucy's spirit exuding love and peace. One day after Mass, she shared this experience with Father Bill. When she related the feeling that came over her at those times and the sense of her mother's presence, she was startled to find out that Father Bill was already aware. That day, he had noticed a radiant blue light near Mary Lou at Mass—the same radiant light that had been near her at Mass ever since her mother's passing.

Ask not ...
Why is this happening?
But rather ...
What is the opportunity?

CHAPTER 41

Embarking on a Mystical Journey

I was leaving for a dinner with David, my thirteen-year-old son. Unbeknownst to him, I had the feeling that we were getting ready to embark on a mystical journey. I suggested we buy some Evian water, bless it with a prayer and love, and then drink it. He looked at me with an amused curiosity and said, "W-h-a-a-a-a-a-t?" My spiritual ideas, or perhaps I should call them quirks, were a never-ending source of entertainment for David.

After stopping at a dingy gas station to buy the water and bless it, I actually kissed my bottle. That was a little much for David. He threw me another look, like "you can't be serious," and then smiled.

For several years, spirituality had been the topic of discussion for David and me. Our Sunday morning breakfasts at one our favorite restaurants often consisted of stacks of golden-brown pancakes, topped with pure maple syrup and a dollop of fresh butter. After eating, we would go for a walk around a large lake at a nearby nature park. Today, however, we were preparing for a new journey.

I was planning to retire from medicine and move onto a purely spiritual path. I was in the process of finishing this book and was also focused on increasing my spiritual energy. I remained uncertain of how closely David's path would be tied to my own, but like the rest of my family, I knew he would be there to help guide me.

At dinner that night, I told David as much. He and his sister would be an integral part of this journey, contributing in meaningful ways to the book and to the spiritual growth of our family.

Raye Ann, my wife, had already played a pivotal role in my journey and with the book by editing numerous early drafts. She had also shown remarkable faith in me. Although she had some doubts about the path I was taking, she chose to stand by my side—to offer as much support as she could muster. I was, and continue to be, most appreciative.

That night as we sat outside at a Cajun seafood restaurant amid flowering plants and trickling fountains, I asked David if he could offer some spiritual insights about this new journey. I excused myself for a few moments to give David some time alone and, on my return, asked him if any thoughts had come to him. He told me that while I was gone he had received a flood of spiritual messages, but he could no longer remember them. He then excused himself and went to the car for something. On his return, I noticed he was carrying a piece of paper and a pen. On the paper he had written three pieces of advice that he felt guided to share with me:

1. *You must prepare for the adventure that is about to be bestowed upon you.*

2. *You must remember in times of hardship that your life is centered on love and spirit.*

3. *You must know what you want in order to achieve your dreams.*

I was amazed at the high level of spiritual direction David was receiving; yet I felt there was still something more he was supposed to tell me. I went to my car and pulled out a ten-inch white candle I had purchased at a local cathedral. As I lit the candle, I told David I thought it might remind him of something else he was to share with me.

He immediately added a fourth piece of advice to his list:

4. *You must be connected with the light of the universe and be able to speak the language that accompanies it.*

He went on to explain that *speak* could mean both to understand and to send out thoughts—to import and export, to receive as well as to radiate.

Over the next several weeks, David and I had many spiritual discussions. He continued to elaborate on his initial guidance. For example, when I asked him, "What is the universal language?" he responded by writing the following: "The inner soul of all humans and animals expressed in an energy that everyone can feel. Human angels can read the language and send out thoughts to help bring all of the troubled humans to love."

Interestingly enough, I was familiar with the term human angel.

To me, the term applies to people who are connected with love and light, who reach out to others with gentleness and beauty. For some, this might be an everyday occurrence, for others, a work in progress; yet at any given point in time, *any one of us* can take on the role of a human angel by simply allowing our essence of love and light to shine forth.

As we begin to see ourselves as human angels, we connect with a higher energy. We come to see ourselves as mystical, beautiful, and loving beings. We strengthen ourselves and radiate our light and love onto others.

I remember the first time I shared my thoughts on human angels with David and my seventeen-year-old daughter, Suzanne. The three of us were having dinner at a restaurant, and I started talking about Anna, our high-school-aged waitress. Anna was exceptionally kind, and as we conversed, she told us that angels had always fascinated her. Furthermore, she mentioned that people often told her that she had an angelic presence. Anna's comments provided the perfect lead-in for our discussion, as she appeared to be a wonderful example of a human angel.

I explained my theory about human angels to Suzanne and David and told them that this was how I viewed each of them. Suzanne identified strongly with what I saying.

Later that night, Suzanne had an unusual experience. While she was driving home, she had a feeling, *a knowing,* that she would be coming upon some deer. She reduced her speed to about twenty miles an hour, causing the car behind her to slow down as well. Within a few minutes, several deer ran in front of her car. Shortly thereafter, a fawn following the first group of deer appeared out of nowhere and managed to pass between the two cars uninjured.

When Suzanne told me the story the next day, I replied that I was quite certain that her experience had taken place because she had come to see herself as a human angel. She had connected with the higher, mystical energy of spirit.

I would often seek out Suzanne's counsel, her spiritual wisdom, as I continued on my spiritual path and encountered an array of challenges, which I might call blessings. Her ability to commune with such heightened energy and light would enable her to provide me with the most comforting of words, the clearest of insights. This precious girl, with whom I feel such an intimate connection, would guide me back to myself, reminding me of my power within, my truth within.

Aside from our talks about human angels, which the three of us engaged in quite often, David and I continued to have many spiritual discussions over breakfasts and dinners. During one such dinner, I asked him how we could come to see the beauty in everyone and everything. Although in the past I had always excused myself as he wrote down his responses to my questions, this time I stayed at the table and read.

When I glanced up, I was taken aback. Like a stenographer in a courtroom, David was writing as he looked upward. Guided in a setting of stillness and faith, he appeared to be in an almost trance-like state. As I peered at the paper, I was surprised to notice that his writing was not only legible but also fairly neat, given that he wasn't even looking at the paper as he wrote. It read, "Beauty is a thing that dwells in all objects, people, animals and plants. Realizing the beauty is seeing beyond what they say and seeing their true inner soul. Once this is realized, words will not need to be spoken—to see how people are and what they feel. You will be able to tell by their radiating energy, from their soul which lies within."

A few weeks later, we took a family vacation to Ocean City, New Jersey, to visit my sister. While there, David purchased an oil painting of two lions sitting side by side. When he showed me the painting and told me the lions reminded him of the two of us, he included this poem which he had written, titled "Lions":

Lions

We are just like two lions sitting side by side
not following normal routines that others abide

The lions are like us sitting in the grass
able to be fierce and strike exceptionally fast

But we know that gentleness is the way of love
just like soaring above as a beautiful dove

The lion is accurate and quick to achieve what it desires
the son looks up to his father as the one he admires

Be strong and agile in all your endeavors
like lions we'll be and our time will be treasured

I was very touched by his poem. The lions in the painting were striking, their eyes so gentle, just as David depicted in his poem. It is a characteristic present in both of our natures.

We returned from Ocean City on a Friday night, and I was scheduled to leave for Lake Tahoe the following Sunday morning. Although I was to attend a medical conference for continuing education, I felt that some meaningful spiritual experience would take place while I was out west. On my return that night, I called the airlines to see if I could get a ticket for David on the off chance he could go with me. I knew Suzanne would not be able to go, since she was to start school the following week. Unfortunately, the flights were all sold out.

Before going to bed that night, David asked me if we could have a spiritual breakfast the next morning. Little did I know where it would lead.

The next chapter is David's recollection.

As evolution has advanced, men have begun to think more intently into the beyond. But the real challenge is not to think, but to live in the beyond, to have the ability to swim in uncharted waters. Whether those waters be cold or choppy, at least one knows that no matter the dynamics of those waters, strength is built, fear is overcome, and miracles are occurring.

—David Sifri, a spiritual communication

CHAPTER 42

Reaching for the Summit
By David Sifri, age fourteen

On our way back from a wonderful vacation to Ocean City, New Jersey, my thoughts were loaded with exotic scenes of unusual events that might take place in the future. I knew my father was going to have an extraordinary, and inspiring, experience on a trip to Lake Tahoe for which he was departing in two days, and I knew that I needed to go with him. Our energy could interfuse to create an overpowering, unstoppable force that would allow us to accomplish our wildest dreams. I could feel the strength of the power that dwelled within me, and it had the intensity of the almighty (God). I truly was inspired to accomplish the impossible!

Later that day, I asked my father if we could have a spiritual breakfast the next morning, and I set the stage for sharing my thoughts about his upcoming trip. Night came and went, and I awoke knowing I couldn't tell him what I was feeling. I did not want to seem clingy and obligate him to invite me to tag along on what I knew would be a life-changing journey. On the way to breakfast, I began to feel depressed, knowing I probably would not be included in the adventure that was about to be bestowed upon my dad.

During our meal, he asked me, "David, how do you feel about me going on this trip?"

"It's fine," I responded, for I was a man of few words.

"This would be too much traveling for you anyway, wouldn't it?" he asked. "I mean, you just got back from a trip, and you start school in a week and a half."

When he said this, I began to realize he might be pondering the same thing that I was. My heart skipped a beat.

"No, I actually really enjoy traveling," I said, almost holding my breath.

My dad paused for a minute, then looked up at the ceiling in a fashion that indicated he was thinking seriously about something.

"Whatcha thinking about?" I asked in a manner that illustrated my awareness of his thoughts.

"Nothing," he said. "Just thinking about walking."

But I knew he was lying. I let it go, though, because I didn't want to compel him to invite me.

"Well, you ready to go?" my dad asked.

"Yeah sure," I said, still holding out hope that he planned to take me with him.

We left the restaurant and headed off to a park we both loved. Near the beginning of our walk, my dad asked me a question that made my spirits jump.

"If I could get you an airline ticket, would you like to go with me on this trip?" he asked.

I smiled broadly and said, "Yeah!" with enthusiasm.

"I'll see if I can get a ticket for you," he said. "I tried last night but didn't have much luck."

My heart was racing with enthusiasm and relief—that I was not going to miss out on something great. My dad called the airlines, and, fortunately, a seat was available. So he booked it for me, and we were scheduled to leave early the next day.

I was awakened the next morning by an annoying beeping sound. It was my alarm clock. I got up and got ready; then we headed off to the airport, where we boarded a flight and took off for Lake Tahoe.

Before we left Cincinnati, my dad told me we would be driving a Toyota sedan with a GPS, which sounded fine. But I asked him, "Do you think we could rent a convertible?"

"Of course, little buddy," he said with a half smile. "I'll see what I can do when we get to Reno."

Once we had landed and retrieved our luggage, I was happy to hear that we would now be driving a Mustang convertible. We picked up the car and were off to our hotel.

The ride to our hotel was absolutely gorgeous. We basked in the beauty of the mountains, which were covered with endless amounts of greenery. It was the kind of beauty that brings a smile to your face. Then we reached the lake. The water was so pure you had to take a second look to make sure your eyes did not deceive you. The crystal-blue water flowed with gentleness and made soft lapping sounds every now and then.

We reached the hotel with our sprits soaring. The room was perfect. It had a beautiful view of the mountains, an abundant amount of space, and a fireplace, which always makes a room feel warm and cozy.

The next day was good. My dad went off to work in the morning. When he was finished, he came back and we went off to lunch. We had a very interesting lunch that day. We talked about how it had been guided that I come on this trip, and how he had picked up on my sense that I should accompany him. Then we came to an understanding that maybe we were speaking the universal language. The universal language is an ability to converse by sending out a certain energy that demonstrates what you're feeling and what you want to explain to a certain person or to other living or nonliving entities.

I then drew him a picture of an image that lay in my head. It was an inspiring picture of two men on a mountain with their hands raised to the heavens. The image depicted humans surrendering to God. It symbolized true faith in God. It was truly a picture of trust.

After lunch, my dad asked me, "What do you want to do this afternoon?"

"I don't care. What do you want to do?" I asked.

"Well, how about we take a little hike in the mountains."

"That sounds good," I said. I was so excited to climb and, perhaps, reach the top where I could surrender to God.

Once we had left the hotel to go climbing in the mountains, we got on a shuttle and headed off to a place where we could climb freely. My adrenaline was rushing from my enthusiasm. It was almost like a desperate need for me to get to the top of the mountain. That striking image of the breathtaking mountain with two men on the top was still in my head, and it kept coming back. This image was extremely empowering. It made my faith just soar exceedingly high.

As the shuttle bus reached a small village, we walked off and gazed upon the mountains that bordered it. We looked around, curious as to where we could find the path we wanted to take. We came to a man who was working in a booth.

"Excuse me," my dad said. "Where can we find this mountain path?" he asked with the gentle tone he always uses, even with strangers, as he pointed to a specific trail on a map.

"Sorry, sir, but this trail is under construction and won't be available."

When I heard him say that, my energy dropped a little bit, because my hopes of climbing to where I had planned started to fade.

"There is another path," the man said, "if you go straight and turn at that big sign." As he said that, he gestured with his hands to show us how to get to the trail.

"Thank you, and have a great day," my father said with the smile that is ever-present on his face.

We walked to the sign, which was about a hundred yards away, and we turned there, only to find a construction site. At that point, I wanted to just turn back because I was fearful of the consequences that might lie ahead for trespassing. But no one said anything to us as we casually strolled right past the construction machinery.

Once we had passed the machinery, I saw the beauty I had come for. Majestic mountains lay in front of us, and we stopped for a minute to gaze upon them. Then we took our first steps onto the path that led up the mountain, unaware of the inspiring, challenging adventure that awaited us.

We started to walk up the dirt trail that stretched before us.

"David," my dad said, "as we walk up this mountain, continue to stay in the moment and gently feel the flowers as you walk by them." He said this in a tone I would describe as soft and sensitive.

"Yeah," I responded. I'm really not much of a talker, but I wanted to let him know that I understood what he was saying.

I took his advice and cleared out any distracting thoughts and just stared at the beauty around me like there was no tomorrow. I was really connected with spirit and with my inner self. I could tell my dad was really in the moment as I watched him sweep his hand over the flowers and even the weeds.

We continued to walk up the path for a while, but the man-made path did not feel right. I can't really describe why it didn't feel spiritual, but it just was not satisfying to me. Apparently my dad was feeling the same way, for he started to wander off the path, heading straight up toward the top of the mountain. I, of course, followed him, for although we look like two different men, our thoughts and energy are surprisingly similar.

The climb started to get steep as we grew closer to the top. We had to grab hold of little bushes to pull ourselves up. I gave thanks to those little plants, for without them we would never have been able to make it up those steep inclines. Eventually, we came to a little trail, which we followed for a while. Then I realized that the trail was not leading in the direction we wanted to head.

"Dad, where is this trail taking us?" I asked with genuine curiosity.

"I don't know where the hell we're going. Do you?" he responded with that sense of humor I love.

"God knows," I answered in my own humorous way.

I started to drift off the small path for a while, and he followed me. It was kind of like we were playing follow the leader, and we each were taking turns being the leader. We came to a rise, where there were two very distinct paths. One looked almost impossible to climb, so we started up the other one. At first we were quickly climbing the path, but it just kept getting steeper and steeper. It was even more challenging, because we both had gym shoes on instead of hiking boots.

At one point, I went to reach up to grip something to pull me up, but I realized there was nothing there to grab. I was stuck in a position where I had no place to go. And if I fell, a fatal drop would await me.

I was scared for my life.

"Dad, I need help! I'm stuck."

"Just hold on a minute, buddy," he said.

When I think back on it now, I think to myself, *How in the world did I hang on?* I was leaning up against a slightly inclined platform and was supporting myself by locking my arm and grasping a root barely below my shoe. The weight of my body was on that arm, and my hand was beginning to sweat. I could feel it slowly starting to slip off my only support.

"Dad, come on! I need some help fast. Please!"

Tears began to fall from my eyes as I said this, for I feared that this may be it for me. I began to think about what all is important in life, such as family and friends. I started to shake and felt unstable. My hand was almost off the root. I was slipping, and my life was at stake.

My dad shouted up to me, "Pray and have faith that God will help us."

"I can't, Dad! I just can't."

I began crying as I finished the last few words, my arms started shaking vigorously, and I thought my life was at its last milestone. What I was unaware of at the time was that my dad was stuck, too. He was barely hanging on with a small toehold and felt that he could fall any minute as well. He had no way of reaching over to where I was. Nor could he climb higher or go down. Upon hearing my words, however, he knew it was now or never. Suddenly, he started climbing up the smooth, steep rock without anything visible to hold on to.

I let go of the root for a second, then immediately grabbed back onto it after seeing my dad's prayer being answered. He began climbing aggressively to a ledge that lay just a few yards away. His faith did not let him down. He reached the ledge with complete success, although his glasses fell off in the process and slid down the mountain and out of his reach. He then grabbed a vine and reached out his hand to help me. I put all my trust in him, released my hand from the root and seized his. When I grabbed his hand, I felt God's ubiquitous presence. My dad pulled me with all his strength to the ledge, where he was standing.

We sat down for a minute and pulled ourselves together, for we both were in great shock. After several minutes, we had recovered, though, and we decided to climb higher. But after climbing up a few yards, we discovered an incredibly dangerous slope that would lead to the top. We debated whether to attempt it or not. Then I realized, whatever you climb up, you have to climb down. Once I thought about that, I immediately declined the option. We then climbed back down the few yards that we had just climbed up.

It was beginning to turn dark, and we had no way of getting down. We thought we would just enjoy the view for a while and be in the moment. But it was hard to do, because large ants would crawl on us, and some of them would bite. After a while, the sun went down, and the moon rose. We walked to a spot on the ledge, where we crawled under a branch and rested our heads. We were going to have to spend the night there, because it was dark and we did not know how to get down. We were stranded.

The spot we chose to lie down in was narrow and close to a fatal drop-off, which I refused to lie near to for fear of rolling off. The temperature began to fall, but we each had a sweater. We put our sweaters on, but we were wearing shorts, so our legs were exceedingly cold. My dad gave up his sweater to me to keep my legs warm. I was greatly thankful but was worried that he would be too cold during the night. I offered it back, but he refused. The sweater did keep me warm, but not as warm as his gentleness and kindness kept my heart.

The night seemed to go on forever. I feared that bears might attack us, because apparently bears came to the village just about every night, and we were close to the village.

My dad and I shivered the whole night as the winds howled through the canyon. It got colder and colder as the night wore on. I woke up several times, and I don't think my dad slept at all.

At around four o'clock in the morning, we started to share spiritual stories, which raised my faith. But it was truly a night from hell.

The sun appeared as dawn was finally approaching. It was a beautiful morning. The sun felt so good against my skin, and I began to warm up. My dad then said, "I don't think we'll be doing *that* again."

When he said that, I thought to myself in a humorous way, *You don't think we'll be staying up here another night? I mean, did you not just sit in that hellhole with me for what felt like forever?*

But instead, I just said, "I know."

By then, the sun was just about fully out, and it seemed to me that my dad was just making himself at home. So I figured I would speak my mind.

"Don't you think we should start heading down?" I said.

"I don't know how we're going to get down," he answered.

He did make a point that neither one of us could see, because he had lost his glasses, and certain circumstances had caused me to discard my contacts. So it would be quite dangerous going down the mountain.

"Well, we might as well find a way, because it's not like it's going to get any easier if we just sit here," I said.

He acknowledged my statement and realized I spoke the truth, so he got up.

"Well, I don't think we should go down the way we came, because that was awful, and it would be twice as hard going back down it," I said. There was another way to get down, but it didn't look promising. It was a ninety-degree drop of uncertain height and had a rock base.

"We'll ask God and see if we should go this way or not," my dad said.

I decided this was a good question, considering none of our options seemed any better than the other. I asked God, and the answer I got back was, "I will guide you through whatever path you choose."

"Dad, I'm not going back the way we came," I said.

"Well, all right then," my dad said. "I guess we'll take this path."

As he said this, he pointed to the path that lay right in front of us.

"Let's go for it," I said.

"Okay," he responded in an uncertain tone.

I went first. I grabbed hold of the edge and hung there. I was scared to let go, for I feared falling and getting injured. Finally, I got up the courage to drop, and I landed safely. Then I slid down, grabbed hold of a bush, pulled myself to the side, and waited for my dad.

His descent was not as graceful.

When he got down off the drop, he slipped and was sliding quickly. As he passed me, I grabbed hold of a little bush and reached out for his hand but was barely able to hold on to it. He stopped, though, and was able to get to where I was.

We slowly proceeded down the mountain and eventually reached the small path we had been on the day before. We walked along that path for a while until we found the village where we had been dropped off and finally arrived safely back at our hotel.

As I reflected back on that appalling night, I realized there was a pure beauty that was present throughout the ordeal. The question was not, was God there talking to us with gentle, loving care? The true question was, were we listening?

So I began to listen, and it was conveyed to me from God that … "Without our strength, we wouldn't have been able to climb the mountain; without our love, we would not have had gentleness with one another, and without our faith, it wouldn't have happened at all."

As we quiet the noise
And go within
Clarity arises

CHAPTER 43

A Ray of Light Pierces the Darkness

I was introduced to Savannah when I ran into Terri, a patient and good friend of mine, at a local restaurant. Unlike Terri's two younger children, who were outgoing and playful, Savannah, who was eight, appeared wonderfully shy. Her quiet manner and soft smile spoke of her innocence as well as her purity. Like an exquisite pearl encased in a protective shell, her spirit was a hidden jewel. As I talked briefly with Savannah during that first meeting, I felt her spirit beckon me. Shortly thereafter, Savannah, Terri, and I had our first lunch together.

It was now a year later, and, once again, I was meeting Terri and Savannah for a light breakfast at a local coffee house. After we exchanged hugs, and Savannah ordered cheesecake, she told me that she had forgotten to bring a picture that she had drawn for me. In the drawing, a turtle was trying to reach an apple on the low-lying branch of a tree. The turtle had placed himself on a hill to get closer to the branch, and the tree was leaning in toward the turtle. Yet as the turtle painfully stretched upward, it was barely able to touch the apple with its long, curly tongue. Behind the hill, the sun was shining brightly, radiating light everywhere. Savannah went on to tell me that in the next scene, a mean hawk would swoop down to snatch the apple away from the turtle, but in the process, the apple would fall and land in the turtle's mouth.

Savannah was very intuitive. Unbeknownst to her, that turtle was me. For the past four months, I had been trying to get that apple down from the branch with little success. I had begun my recent journey with the expectation of being able to reach the apple without too much difficulty, of mistakenly predicting how and when the apple would fall. I had never considered that I might obtain the apple only through the help of outside forces when I was least expecting it. At times, I also failed to realize how much God was bending that tree, how much he was helping to guide me.

Four months earlier, 1 had retired from my medical practice to pursue writing and other spiritual endeavors. I left my practice with certain expectations: I would continue to climb higher and higher on my spiritual path, enjoying a grander view of life every step of the way; this book, by some miraculous feat, would be finished and out in huge numbers by Christmas of 2007; and I would continue to have frequent spiritual lunches with friends and acquaintances, experiencing the bliss of this communion of spirit.

None of this was to be true. I did leave my practice in early August 2007, and I began the spiritual adventure of a lifetime, but it was not at all as I had expected. It was to be a faith-based journey, and I had much to learn. Through my constant struggles I would come to understand that great faith meant continuing to believe in God despite all evidence to the contrary, particularly when God appeared to be quiet, absent, or distant; it meant maintaining that faith in the most uncomfortable of situations—situations that I had been led to through spiritual guidance.

This was somewhat different from simply finding myself in challenging circumstances and leaning on faith. During the past six years, I had experienced many challenging events in my life and had found my faith to be a continual source of comfort and inspiration. In one such instance, I had witnessed my father being wheeled out of a cardiac-procedure room toward my family when he was already clinically dead, a fact of which neither the doctors nor the nurses were aware. As my mother leaned over to stroke his face and kiss him, she sensed that something was wrong. When I moved in closer, I noticed that he was cold, clammy, and still. He wasn't breathing, and he had no pulse. We alerted the nurses, and the doctors immediately called a code. Within seconds, my father was back in the procedure room. Forty-five minutes later, the staff came out to tell us they had been unable to revive him.

Later that night, my brother was rushed to the emergency room after collapsing in the hospital elevator with crushing chest pain. Although he and my mother would be grief-stricken for some time to come, I felt at peace with my father's death, knowing that he had returned home, that those doctors and nurses had tried their best, and that he would always be with me.

My faith would carry me through a challenging time once again when I watched my wife endure an intense regimen of radiation and chemotherapy for cancer. I remember a particularly difficult week, when Raye Ann was extremely weak and bedridden. At the same time, my daughter, Suzanne, was experiencing intense abdominal pain and a high fever. Although Raye Ann wanted to care for her, she was barely able to function herself. My wife's family was there, offering support in many ways. Yet, as a father and a husband, I wanted to comfort my wife and my daughter in the most personal of ways. During that long one-week period, I didn't know where to focus my attention. They were both struggling immensely. I thought to myself, *How much more can I take?* But my faith remained strong. I knew that God was with me.

Perhaps my greatest challenge of faith was surrendering my son, David, to God. A number of years ago, when David was nine, it was spiritually communicated to me that he would be dying soon—an event that of course never took place. The communication started gradually, like a seed being planted. I would open a spiritual text, and as I began to read, I would get the feeling that something was going to happen to David. Over time, that seed sprouted and began to grow, and I began to have a strong sense that David's time on this earth was limited.

My initial reaction was confusion and denial. What was going on? Was my mind playing tricks on me? Certainly I couldn't be losing my sweet son at such a tender age, but as time went by, the feeling deepened. I continued to question myself, asking whether the feeling was real. But in my heart I knew it was. I was being forewarned.

The communication first came to me several weeks before Christmas. I remember thinking that by the following Christmas, David would not be with us. He would not be there to unwrap his presents, to open his stocking. I was overwrought with emotion, wondering how I could deal with his absence. I would miss him terribly—his gentle nature, his soft kisses, the way he rubbed my ear at night. Yet I had such faith in God, such warm and tender feelings, that I knew if David were being called home, there was a good reason. He would be returning to his holy Father in a placed filled with absolute love and peace, a place where he belonged. In some ways I was not surprised by the communication. David had always seemed too sensitive and innocent for this world—too angelic.

From a spiritual perspective, I was ready to release David, to completely surrender and place him into God's hands, but from a more human perspective, my heart was torn. I knew I would miss David beyond measure. I would miss stroking his face, holding him close, snuggling with him as I put him to bed. He was such an intimate part of me.

I remember giving a talk on hypertension one evening to a couple of doctors and their wives at a seafood restaurant that overlooked the Ohio River. As I talked with one of the women, who was surely a human angel, tears began streaming down my face as I told her what I was experiencing. It was an emotional night for me, but we had the most beautiful spiritual discussion. I felt such love from her and her husband.

Eventually, I began asking David about his favorite music and clothes. I was beginning to prepare for his funeral. In my mind, I was planning the eulogy; my focus would be on the wonder of spirit—the importance of faith—the beauty of God. Spiritually I knew David would always be with me, as close to me as my own breath. I was coming to find peace with the situation.

Like most mothers, my wife's greatest fear has always been losing a child. The mere idea of such an immense loss was almost incomprehensible, but as I continued to experience this overwhelming communication, I knew I had to tell her. I didn't want her to be caught unaware.

I began to share with Raye Ann my feeling that David would be dying soon. Initially she just listened. My comments caused her some anxiety, but she wasn't ready to fully incorporate them into her world. As my feeling intensified, however, I became more vocal as to what I felt was going to happen. Ever so slowly, it started to sink in. She would be losing her son—and losing him soon.

I could feel the tension rising within Raye Ann. Although I tried to be very calm and to stress the spiritual aspect of what might happen, Raye Ann's mind was racing. She could not seriously consider the possibility of David dying. Her brain was functioning like a circuit breaker; it was working to prevent an overload. Although her faith was strong, this would be too much. My wife, who had long struggled with depression, told me she simply wouldn't be able to handle David's death. It would destroy her.

I decided it was time to have a conversation with God. As I walked out into the night air, amid the sparkling stars and the wandering clouds, a felt a certain peace and began to speak.

I had not previously had this conversation with God because I had so much faith in him—so much trust. If David needed to return home, I knew there was a reason. Now, however, things were different. Something new had been added to the equation. As I expressed this to God, I told him I had complete faith in him and would accept whatever he chose to do. He needed to understand, however, the immense impact that David's death would have on my wife. She would lose her sanity.

As soon as I expressed my concern, something changed. The feeling that my son would be dying immediately vanished.

In that moment, I knew that David would be fine. I couldn't believe it!

I hurried back into the house and found Raye Ann in the bedroom. I went up to her, took her hands in mine, and told her she needn't worry about David; everything would be all right. When I explained what had happened, a tender smile spread across her face, and tears of joy filled her eyes. The heaviness, which just moments before had draped the room, was gone. In its place was an overwhelming feeling of warmth and heartfelt appreciation.

In the following months, I wondered whether the spiritual communication had all been in my mind. Had I simply imagined it? Then one day, as I reviewed a study on sudden infant death syndrome, I learned that many parents who had lost a child to SIDS had a feeling their child would be dying before it actually happened. At that moment, I knew my sense of David's impending death had been real.

Several years later, during an intimate spiritual conversation with David, I told him of my experience, of how I had felt certain that he was going to die. As he gazed at me with his big brown eyes, he said quietly, "I knew I was going to die too." When I asked him for details, he grew silent. It wasn't something he was ready to talk about.

When he was in the eighth grade, David decided to leave his middle school to pursue home schooling in order to write and travel with me. While my wife fretted over his decision, she received the following spiritual communication: *You need not fear David's decision. He isn't supposed to be here anyway—everything he is experiencing is "gravy."*

During all of these events, my faith never wavered. As a matter of fact, it was my faith that enabled me to soar, to grow closer to God.

Now, however, things would change. David and I would soon attempt to do something outside the normal human realm.

I have always felt a strong connection with Christ. Even when I was an agnostic, I felt the values and love that Jesus espoused were of the highest magnitude. David has felt a very close bond to Christ as well. It is a bond that transcends religion—one that focuses on light and love, on our oneness with spirit.

During the past several years, I have become increasingly aware of the light and love inside of me and have tried to build upon it. I have also become more aware of the limitless nature of faith. As Jesus stated, "Ask, and it will be given you; seek, and you will find; knock, and it will be opened to you" (Mathew 7:7 NKJV).

Inspired by such beautiful words, David and I set out to achieve the highest level of light and love that was humanly possible—to pierce the barrier that existed between heaven and earth, one that few were aware of and even fewer had broken. As we attempted to pierce this barrier, we would invite the most challenging of faith-based experiences. In so doing, our faith would be tested in ways we never dreamed possible. This would be the most difficult experience of our lives.

This faith-based journey began with the experience on the mountain of which David wrote in the previous chapter. When we approached the mountaintop that day, it was with the understanding that we were seeking something greater. We were searching for a spiritual breakthrough, attempting to achieve the impossible.

As we set out on our climb, there was no indication of the difficulties that lay ahead, only reassuring signs of God's presence. Yet I would discover later, during our struggles, that those signs were easily forgotten.

When we started our climb, it was warm and sunny. We eventually left the path to forge our own trail. After working our way up the mountainside, we gradually found ourselves on the slanted slope of a big rock, one with little to hold on to. Making matters worse, we weren't adequately prepared to climb. We both wore tennis shoes, we had no ropes or climbing equipment, and we carried only a backpack filled with two sweaters and two small bottles of water.

When David told me he couldn't hold on much longer, as he supported himself solely by holding on to a small root with one hand, I knew something had to be done. I suggested we pray. Although I was barely holding on myself and could neither see nor feel anything to pull myself up with, I felt God encouraging me to take a leap of faith. I pushed off the toehold, and with nothing visible to hold onto, I reached out onto the steeply inclined rock. My heart was pounding as I clawed at the smooth surface. I was acutely aware that I was in a most vulnerable position, that I might fall at any moment.

But against all odds, I began to move upwards.

It was nothing short of a miracle. In less than a minute, I had advanced to the top of the slope and was able to help David.

As I stretched downward to pull David up, my glasses slipped off and fell into the ravine. Without them, I was almost blind; everything was a blur. But that didn't matter. I was ecstatic to have reached David and most thankful for the miracle that had occurred. We had asked God for help in the direst of circumstances, and he had encouraged us to step out through faith into the seemingly impossible.

Dusk began to give way to darkness, and David and I had to make a decision. We were stranded on a narrow ledge and needed to determine whether we would spend the night on the mountain or try to climb down. We knew we couldn't get back the way we came, and there were no clear alternatives.

We had come up the mountainside to achieve something greater, to begin a journey into the unknown. We felt the need to ask for guidance and to understand how to achieve the impossible—to break the barrier that existed between heaven and earth.

We sought to fully surrender, to fully awaken, to the light of

God—to experience oneness with all, love with all, on earth as it is in heaven.

After only a moment's consideration, we decided to stay on the mountainside. Months later, I would discover that David would have been more than happy to head down the mountain that night and climb into his warm bed, but he said nothing. When I suggested we stay, he quickly assented. He had absolute faith in me ... and in God.

By then it was getting colder, and the winds were picking up. David's shorts were paper thin, and he was starting to shiver. I suggested he wear my sweater as pants, both arms of the sweater stretching over his legs while the body of it covered his waist. Although he was reluctant to take the sweater, he finally acquiesced. I was relieved. It was much easier for me to deal with the cold than to watch my son shivering.

After a while, we decided to lie down and get some sleep. As we lay on the rocks, using pinecones for a pillow, the temperature dropped, and the wind picked up. Swarms of biting ants, nearly an inch in length, began to crawl on us. For the next several hours, we were overrun by these six-legged creatures as they wandered up our legs, under our shorts, and across our arms. We were pulling one off of us every thirty seconds. There was no stopping them.

Several hours later, they retreated. By that time, it was bitter cold, and the winds were howling. I didn't stop shivering for the rest of the night.

Around three in the morning, by my internal clock, I asked David if perhaps we might talk since neither one of us was sleeping anyway. We began discussing inspirational books we had read, prayers we found to be especially meaningful, and our spiritual thoughts in general. For the next three hours, we shared these ideas and prayed together. I was feeling good. Even though it had been a difficult night, our faith remained strong as we turned to God during this challenging period. Although we didn't have a functioning clock, I knew it was approaching 6:00 a.m. It was time for the sun to rise.

I continued to watch for the morning light while reassuring David that it wouldn't be much longer, but the light didn't come. Instead of the dawn, we experienced only infinite blackness. Meanwhile the temperature continued to drop, and the winds became increasingly fierce. I couldn't understand what was going on. Where was the sun? Why wouldn't the dawn appear? As the minutes slowly ticked past, I began to get angry.

We had been guided by God to stay on this mountain. We had endured the dark, bitter-cold night with faith and prayer. We had traversed the course. Now, though, instead of crossing the finish line, we found ourselves freezing, exhausted, and confused in this no-man's land. The rules had changed. We were no longer experiencing time in the normal realm. Time had slowed to a crawl. While I awaited God's response to my questions, I felt nothing—no encouraging words, no comforting signs—only emptiness.

For the first time in my life, I began to accuse God of being insensitive, of leading us down a path and then abandoning us. Where was his gentleness? Where was his compassion?

As I reflected on the events of the night, it occurred to me that perhaps it wasn't God who had guided us on this path. Perhaps it was some other power, some negative-energy source. What the hell was going on?

Until now I had always been the one with the answers, with undying faith, the person others came to when life proved too difficult, when they had given up hope ... but now it was I who was in despair. I found myself questioning my beliefs, questioning God. As the night wore on, time hung lifeless in the void. I was miserable, trapped in a disturbing dream, robbed of the promise of morning light.

The darkness seemed to continue forever. I sat there freezing in a T-shirt and shorts, surrounded by a vast emptiness filled only with silence. As I shook uncontrollably for hours on end, I found myself abandoning all hope.

During this time, David would sleep lightly and occasionally awaken. He, too, was cold and hungry. Although he now had two sweaters, he was five foot ten and 130 pounds. He had very little insulation. While I could cope with my own suffering, his was another matter.

Six hours later, by my internal clock, the first light finally began to appear. As the sun's rays filtered through the darkness, I started to feel better. And although I had suffered—like I had never suffered before—hope and faith began to reemerge.

Once again, we reached out for God's voice. We asked him how we had done, and David shared God's soft, loving reply with me: "Your faith wavered, but your objective did not."

Over the next few hours, I would try to make sense of it all. I was upset that my faith had wavered. I'd always had such high expectations of myself, but as I thought about it, I couldn't imagine why my faith wouldn't have been shaken under such circumstances. As I continued to contemplate the experience, I came to an understanding. To break the barrier would take immeasurable faith—blind faith that persisted even when God was silent and had led us into the worst of circumstances. It all started to make sense. *The only way to understand that level of faith was to experience it.* This was the level of faith it would take to achieve the impossible—the level of faith of which Christ had spoken. How could it be otherwise?

Later that day, we would ask God, "If our faith had been greater, would our experience have been better?"

His response was, "It would have been the same. I guided you to that experience to show you how great your faith was. I know you suffered through the night, but I think it was worth it; just to tell you, I suffered through it with you. I thought it was worth it, but you can make your own decision."

I came to understand the absolute love and strength that God possessed. To have led us up that mountain and to have watched us suffer as he grew silent, so we could pursue our dream to fully surrender—to fully awaken—to his ever transcendent light, was truly remarkable.

I also came to realize that God was trying to remind us of our inner strength when we were on the mountaintop. He had more faith in us than we had in ourselves. That is why he guided David and me into such a difficult situation—why he took us to the brink. He knew we were capable of so much more than we had ever imagined, and now he would invite us to discover it—"to conquer the limits of ourselves."

We had chosen this most challenging yet fruitful of paths, one laden with opportunities and communion. Our ever-loving God was there to guide us, to sacrifice for us, so we could experience a life beyond our wildest imaginations. We would be in this together, every step of the way.

The next morning, David and I rode our bikes along mountain trails and then into the area surrounding Lake Tahoe, finally stopping at a restaurant for lunch. As we sat on the patio, with the lake's translucent blue water and encasing mountains in full view, we were on an absolute high. During this time, we conversed with God and came to appreciate and experience him in a whole new dimension. In response to one of our questions, he said, "I am here to serve. As I give you guidance and you follow it, it amazes me to see the beauty in the way the human thinks. Your life is my life. I will always treat you as I do myself. My heart is your heart, my breath is your breath, my love is your love."

He spoke of the importance of self-love, of blessing ourselves. When we asked him how we should bless ourselves, he said, "The same way you would bless others, by connecting with love and sending positive energy to yourself. People never think of blessing themselves, but what they don't realize is they need it the most."

After we finished our lunch, Vince, our kind and attentive waiter, asked us what we had planned for the next few days. We told him we intended to pierce the barrier, the one that existed between heaven and earth.

Vince looked at us for a moment, smiled, and said, "I am not religious, but I know what you mean. I wish you the best. I occasionally get the feeling to dive ten feet into the depths of Lake Tahoe and take a big gulp of water.

"As I drink the pure water, I experience heaven on earth."

Upon leaving the restaurant and reflecting on Vince's words, I was reminded of the universal language of spirit, of love that knows no boundaries.

Over the next two months, David and I continued our climb of a very steep mountain. It was a journey that required our undivided attention. As we ascended into the clouds, we grew confused by the absence of landmarks, the thin air. We lost sight of our selves and our truths. We searched for the light but couldn't see. We walked with faith but often stumbled. We grew angry, tired, and disillusioned ...

And yet with every fall came fresh resolve.

At other times, however, we experienced pure bliss. The clouds would clear, and we saw and felt God as never before. We came to better understand his humility, his selflessness, and his unending love as he guided us with inspiration and spoke to us with love and tenderness.

In all circumstances there is challenge, in all moments there is loudness, and in all places there is darkness. Through love, there is release of all.

On October 23, we reached the summit—weak, confused, and uncertain. Three very good friends came to Chicago to be with David and me on this special day. They had such faith in us. They had come to welcome us back from the stormy seas, to remind us of who we were, and to shower us with love. We had been told for many months: "On October 23, a miracle will occur which will cause the blind to see."

The kingdom of God is within you.

—Luke 17:21 NIV

CHAPTER 44

And the Truth Shall Set You Free

By David Sifri, age fourteen

Since early 2007, my dad and I had a strong internal sense that something astonishing would transpire on October 23. We expected a miracle beyond anyone's imagination. Somehow, we thought this miracle might include an appearance on *The Oprah Winfrey Show*, which of course seemed completely implausible. But it's what we thought, and we were sticking to it, no matter what other people said.

When October 23 arrived, my dad and I were in Chicago, getting ready to leave our hotel room to meet three of his friends for an afternoon adventure. These three women—Barb, Ellen, and Sue—came all the way from Cincinnati because of their passionate support and faith in us—faith that we would have a remarkable experience on this day. They were absolutely incredible people.

We all met in the lobby and debated where to go. Then Ellen remembered hearing church bells earlier that morning and was led by her intuition to follow them. So we did just that. I trusted that she had a true spiritual connection. She pointed in the general direction from which the church bells had come. My dad took over from there. He tuned in to energy, which was to guide him through the streets.

He would at times walk into oncoming traffic, and we would cease to follow him for fear of death. He, on the other hand, had no such fear. This worried us all the more.

Eventually we came upon a Catholic church, St. Peter's in the Loop, and we all went in. There was a church service in progress, so we proceeded to the balcony to listen to the rest of the Mass. What struck my father the most was how devoted all the listeners were—how focused they appeared to be on the service. I was impressed by their expressions of love toward Jesus, Mary, and the disciples as they kissed their statutes on their foreheads, knelt down in front of them, and prayed. It was a Tuesday morning, not a typical day for service; these parishioners were not attending out of a sense of obligation.

After the Mass ended, we all went down to light a candle. At first we lit separate candles, and then we decided to all light one at the same time. My dad counted up from one, and on three we all lit one.

We then left the church and started walking down the street. My dad had a feeling that we should go into a pizza place that we passed on the right. As we went in, a very kind man greeted us with a big smile on his face. We said we needed a table for five, and he looked around and saw that there was only a small circular table and two-top table available. Any other manager might have waited until an open table became available, but he moved two people from a four-top and placed them at the circular table. He then scooted the four-top together with the two-top and sat us there. The manager then smiled at us and said in a joking way, "Who comes in here with five people? I mean it's just such a weird number." We all laughed, and he continued to make similar humorous remarks throughout the meal. When one of us went to the restroom, he remarked, "Where's that fifth wheel gone to?"

As we began to look over the lunch menu, I noticed something ironic. Under the choices for pizzas, it said, "Number One Thin Crust Pizza recommended by *The Oprah Winfrey Show*." Given our Oprah connection, all of us found that intriguing. After we ordered our pizza, I began to enlighten the others about a dream that I had experienced the previous night. I had dreamed that we had run into Oprah on the street, and she invited us to her gorgeous house, where we talked over dinner and discussed being on her show. It was a very inspirational dream but a situation I thought had little chance of happening.

Near the end of our lunch, Barb suggested we walk down to Oprah's studio. The idea exhilarated all of us and gave us some hope of possibly meeting Oprah. So we went down to the studio, then broke up into separate parties to try to cover the whole building. I felt like a fool stalking this innocent celebrity, but at the same time, it was invigorating.

Ellen, this small force of a woman, was the first to try to gain entry into the highly protected facility. She approached the front entrance and asked to speak with someone in charge but was denied entry. She moved on to the side door and was able to get inside. I saw her grin slightly; however, her success was short-lived, for when I looked around, she was back on the street where she had started. I could not help but smile and laugh a little. She was a persistent woman, a trait that would serve her well.

As time passed, and we waited for Oprah to leave her studio, I started to feel that this was just a waste of time. Eventually we just gave up and headed back to the hotel.

After returning to the hotel, I flopped onto the bed and moaned about the day being a complete failure. I then jokingly wrote on a piece of paper "Oct. 23 = dud" and gave it to my dad. He laughed at it and said the day wasn't over yet.

The five of us went on to have a great evening, taking in the beautiful scenery on the cool, clear night. We looked out onto the lush parks and over the surrounding sparkling lights of the bountiful city. The wind felt soft and smooth as it brushed against my face and filled me with an inner peace. We then had an amazing and quite unexpected formal dinner overlooking Lake Michigan and the marina. The women were hesitant to order anything but side dishes at the restaurant because of the exorbitant prices. They were having trouble incorporating the idea of abundance into their daily lives. So they ordered three side dishes to share among themselves. I was the only one to order a real entree.

During dinner, we began talking about the October 23 date and what it might have meant. We were all confused about the significance of this particular date. So far nothing unusual had occurred. Then Ellen brought up a very interesting idea. She said that even though we might not be aware of it yet, she knew that somewhere, somehow, a miracle had indeed happened on this day. My dad and I really liked that idea, because it gave us hope and faith that a miracle had in fact taken place.

The next day, we all left Chicago and headed home to Cincinnati.

About a month and a half later, my dad asked me if I would be interested in writing another story for this book. I found the idea quite spectacular, for I wanted to become more involved in the book, which was going to change the lives of many. He asked me if I had a story in mind. As I thought back over the last few months, I remembered having an extraordinary experience that I had somehow forgotten. As we talked, we came to realize that I'd had that experience on a Tuesday in Chicago. Then it dawned on me that it had been Tuesday the twenty-third of October …

I had started out that day with an intense feeling of inner love and beauty. It was a cold, damp day in Chicago. The winds were blowing, and it was beautiful in its own distinctive fashion. My thoughts were at ease, my heart was centered, and all was still. When my dad and I met his friends that morning, we said our usual hellos and gave them all a hug. Then we started our breakfast with an exceptional discussion. I could feel the presence of the remarkable energy that we were all radiating without realizing it. We helped ourselves to the buffet that lay before us. As I ate my meal, I treasured every bite of food as if it were my last. As I savored each bite, I could taste the intense nutrients and energy the food was supplying me. I gave appreciation to the food and felt a strong energy in return.

While the others were talking, I glanced out the window. I noticed a tree blowing in the wind—moving swiftly and smoothly, basically surrendering and allowing the wind to control its every movement. In that precise second, all things became distorted. I was unaware of what was happening. I could experience the beautiful emotions and purity that the tree felt. I could sense the dynamic soul that lay within it. I felt as if I were floating, unrestrained by my earthly emotions, and it felt exceedingly spectacular. All of my senses were heightened, and I could focus on important events that were taking place. I could hear the sounds of nature and beauty. It was as if all things were moving in slow motion. I was keenly aware of everything that was going on: a car driving past, the waiter taking our dishes, the trees swaying in the wind—all in the same instant.

As I observed everything in slow motion, I was in the moment completely. All my thoughts had quieted, and I was unquestionably in a state of absolute purity. As I looked outside, I saw beauty in everything, whether or not it was alive. Every barrier seemed climbable, clearing all obstacles seemed effortless, and the impossible seemed definitely possible. Christ must have felt this energy when he was alive, this feeling of control—and yet a willingness to surrender, a feeling of infinite tranquility. He must have united with this miraculous energy of excellence to perform the miracles he did. I was inspired to accomplish my dreams and to attain the impossible, even if it meant climbing the highest mountain, because I was moving with blind faith, and I was happy to admit it.

With all the beauty that I felt around me, nothing could lower my energy. I could take the positive out of every comment made and all actions in motion. Everything made me smile. I began to appreciate it all. I realized that this was how I wanted to feel all the time. I wanted to be uplifted every day and never experience any negative energy.

I had myself to thank for this extraordinary experience with which I was blessed. My thoughts and positive outlook on that day had allowed this unforgettable experience to occur. God definitely played an important role, but *I created the experience*. Therefore, it was important to thank myself for the experience. When you begin to realize that you make your experiences happen, you begin to have a greater appreciation for yourself. And this causes your energy to rise.

The energy that I connected with that day was the energy of the soul of God. It was energy so pure, innocent, and gentle that when you experience it, tears fall from your eyes.

Now you may be asking how someone could have forgotten such a powerful experience. I don't have an answer to that question. The important thing is that it in fact did happen. And even without the answers to such questions, I can still appreciate the true pure beauty of this experience, which provided me with growth and a deeper understanding of the spiritual world.

Most of all, as I came to better understand my truth, it moved me one step closer to accomplishing my dream!

Seize the moment
And feel the spirit of life

FINAL THOUGHT

It all begins with awareness.

When we realize that each moment in our lives is precious and sacred, we truly start to live. We are less likely to be distracted by the noise of daily living and more likely to focus our attention on our senses and our energy.

We come to treasure every moment of our lives as we create ourselves anew with the understanding that we are a living, evolving, spiritual energy here on earth for a short period of time to experience whatever we desire.

As we proceed along this path, we come to feel life's pulsating energy within ourselves and those around us. We move into a dimension of spiritual awareness defined by love, peace, and joy. It is a dimension in which we are aware of our eternal existence, a dimension in which we celebrate our being, and a dimension in which our oneness with God and spiritual love is ever present, ever appreciated, and ever more.

For we are
And ever will be
Love

ABOUT THE AUTHOR

George Sifri earned medical and law degrees from The Ohio State University and completed an internal medicine residency at Vanderbilt University. His professional interests and seminar presentations focus on healing through spirituality.

David Sifri earned his bachelor's degree at the University of Miami. He is pursuing postgraduate studies in psychology.

Made in the USA
Lexington, KY
20 November 2016